Dear Mad'm

Dear Mad'm

Stella Walthall Patterson

Drawings by Alice Harvey

Cover drawing by Vivian Witt

Books for a better world

Naturegraph Publishers, Inc.
Happy Camp, California

Library of Congress Cataloging-in-Publication Data

Patterson, Stella Walthall, 1866-1956
  Dear Mad'm.

    Reprint. Originally published: New York:
Norton, 1956.
    1. Patterson, Stella Walthall, 1866-1956.
2. California—Biography. 3. Mountain life—
California. I. Title. II. Title: Dear Madam.
CT275.P465A3 1982 979.4'05'0924 [B] 82-22432
ISBN 978-087961-131-6
ISBN 0-87961-131-6

Naturegraph Publishers has been publishing books on
natural history, Native Americans, and outdoor subjects since
1946. Free catalog available

Books for a better world

Naturegraph Publishers, Inc.
PO Box 1047 ● 3543 Indian Creek Rd.
Happy Camp, CA 96039
(530) 493-5353
www.naturegraph.com

Stella Walthall Patterson (Dear Mad'm)
Photo courtesy *Pioneer Press*

Are you curious to know more about "Dear Mad'm" who was Stella Walthall Patterson? After reading my grandmother's copy of *Dear Mad'm*, my wife, Elizabeth, and I decided to include Stella in our ongoing search into our families' histories. The more we learned, the more interesting she became! We are writing a short history about my great-aunt, now known as Dear Mad'm, who lived a fascinating life, even before moving to a remote mountain mining claim to write her famous book. She came from a prominent pioneer family, was orphaned at seven, was a young artist in Paris, a writer, and a music teacher in California. She was a wife first to a noted San Francisco judge, and later to a young, rugged rancher. During our quest, we have met many wonderful people we call "Friends of Stella", and have received great encouragement and information. We trust you will find her life as interesting and intriguing as we have, and that our book will answer many of the questions over which readers of *Dear Mad'm* have pondered. Watch for *Dear Mad'm, Who Was She?* to be published by Naturegraph in the fall of 2010.

Peter and Elizabeth Walthall Lismer

One

A PRETTY, serene-faced Sister came to my hospital room and took me in a wheel chair to the cubicle where X-rays were to be taken of my injured leg. When the older Sister in charge there had finished the task, she patted me kindly.

"You have young legs," she said.

She started something.

That I should have anything young was astonishing. And my vanity was tickled, legs being a fetish in the land at this time. I began thinking of things I might do on my young legs. The result was that as soon as I was told that my leg was only bruised, I left the hospital and returned to my friend's home where I was visiting, in the pretty little town of Arcata on the coast of Northern California.

The following morning I sat in a big, comfortable chair, my bandaged right foot and leg propped up before me, staring at a calendar on the wall. It was the fourteenth of April, a day remarkable for one reason only—it was my birthday. I was eighty years old.

In my youth I thought that any woman who lived to be eighty must be in her second childhood, or at least tottering on the edge of the grave. But I had always felt young, and lately I have had to be pretty careful not to act as young as I felt. Of course I knew that some of my friends spoke of me as "old Mrs. Patterson," and marveled at the way I hung on to life—the dull, just-waiting sort of life of an old woman—as they saw it. My friends were a charming group, but the most intelligent of friends are likely to think everything is over for a woman of eighty.

I might have agreed with them indefinitely if I hadn't, the month before, left my little home in San Francisco and come up here to visit my friend in Arcata. One day I accompanied a group of people on a picnic in the Klamath Forest and tripped over a wire. My leg seemed to be quite badly hurt, and my alarmed friends rushed me to the hospital. The injury was actually unimportant, as the X-ray showed.

Now, back in my friend's house, I had time to think. I began by considering what I might do on my young legs. Why be sticking around, waiting to be carried out feet first, when I could be stepping out like a young thing, having fun in the land of the living? First of all, I decided, I wanted freedom. Freedom to do just as I pleased, wear my hair in a tight biddy knot, my skirts too long, my shoes too large and too flat. I wanted to stoop if I wanted to, without having someone say, "Dear, it makes you look so old to stoop." Or, "Darling, don't wrinkle your nose and peer around—it makes you look so quaint." Or "Don't you think you should reduce twenty or thirty pounds?"

A plan began to formulate in my mind. I determined to embark on an adventure of living alone at eighty. And I would do this in a cabin I had bought two years before as part of an "investment" in a placer mining claim in the mountains overlooking the Klamath River, about a hundred miles from a railroad. I and three of my friends who knew no more about placer mining than I did—which was nothing whatever—bought adjoining claims. I had done nothing more about mine except to make sure the assessment work required by law was done each year, the first of July being the legal deadline. The State of California said that unless one hundred dollars' worth of improvements were made each year on every mining claim, that claim was forfeited and someone else could take possession of it.

I had placed this matter of assessment work on my claim in the capable hands of a reliable young man and his partner who owned—and worked—placer claims adjacent to mine. Each time July rolled around, they had fulfilled their contract with me, sent a proper report to the California State Bureau of Mines—in short, they took care of everything. What my friends did about their assessment work I did not know, as they had moved to distant places and I had lost track of them.

Actually, there was no valid reason for my going to live on my claim—but I had to have some excuse other than my desire for freedom to do as I please and an insistent longing to follow the beckoning finger of adventure before it was too late. And I have learned that if you say you have to do even the maddest thing "for business reasons" people will nod in agreement, while if you say you're doing it for no reason on earth except that you want to, impassioned objections will be voiced.

I refused to face the fact that when I had visited my cabin for the first and last time two years before, I was told that my nearest neighbor, an eccentric character, lived a mile and a half away. The young men who took care of my claim had a cabin on a lake five miles distant and drove back and forth to work every day. How wonderful would it be, I thought, to do exactly as I pleased, see no one for days at a time—maybe even weeks. I would try it for a year, I promised myself bravely. Then, if I didn't like it, I could return to my cushioned, old-ladyish life in San Francisco under the lovingly solicitous eyes of relatives and friends.

Soon my leg was usable again. Then I became as busy as an old hen digging out sprouting seeds from a garden. And speaking of gardens, one of the principal items of my plan was the growing of flowers in a garden made with my own hands. This had been a secretly cherished ambition since my childhood, when I had grown sickly radishes in a corner of the family garden that even the old hens refused to eat.

With the thought of that flower garden mushrooming in my mind, I walked the two blocks to the post office—hardly limping at all by this time. There I bought twenty post cards. Standing at the high, ink-marred desk I wrote ten requests for seed catalogues to as many firms. The rest of the post cards I sent to close relatives and friends, telling them as casually as possible what I was about to do.

I stood for several minutes chewing the stub of my pencil—

not for me those unpredictable post-office pens. Apparently, I was deep in thought, but actually I was just plain stumped. What address should I give all these people? What was the name of the post office nearest to my cabin? I decided it must be Happy Camp. No, I didn't make up that name. You can find it on any good map of California. I scrawled Happy Camp on the post cards and dropped them in the mail slot. Then I went blissfully out to buy groceries at the one big general-merchandise store in the town.

They caught me coming and they caught me going in that fine store. As I went in I filled a carton with various items from the grocery shelves. As I turned to go out, I saw a whole department given over to seeds and bulbs. Why wait to hear from the seed companies? I could supplement my supply of seeds from them later. I went on a buying spree that left my purse as flat as the proverbial pancake. There were stands and stands displaying bright-colored little packages of seed and trays and trays of plump bulbs. I scooped the trays bare and started in on the seed packages. Nothing could stop me, not even the disapproving looks of the young clerk who followed me about apprehensively.

I bought everything from hyacinths to Dutch iris bulbs, and added a miscellaneous collection of little knobby things that I had no name for. Each bulb was concentrated youth that turned my soul topsy-turvy. I rifled the flower-seed stands, buying everything from baby's breath to castor beans. I also bought two pairs of garden gloves, a floppy bright green garden hat, a flamingo-pink garden smock, a pair of kneepads and several small gadgets I saw in the showcase, but didn't stop to figure out just what they would be used for.

I was a little troubled when I saw the size of my box of garden supplies. It was a good four times as large as my box of groceries. Well, nothing I could do about that now, as all my money was gone, except what was required for my bus ticket.

I packed my suitcase, put on a discreet amount of powder, lipstick and rouge, and a very becoming hat with a veil. All of which made me look younger than I am. Particularly the mesh veil that I had over my hat and swathed around my throat, concealing nicely its wintry look. Saying goodbye to my friend, I took a taxi to the bus station, where I assembled my belongings and bought a ticket to Willow Creek, thereby sealing my fate. At Willow Creek I would catch a mail stage, which would take me to my cabin. I boarded a small local bus and traveled thirty-five miles inland through precipitous tree-covered mountains to the hamlet of Willow Creek.

There I found Tom, the driver of the mail truck, who would —I hoped—carry me safely to my destination. Tom eyed me with patient, disinterested tolerance. Carrying mail was his business, not carrying passengers. However, his manner implied, he couldn't leave me stranded, so what couldn't be cured must be endured.

He opened the door of the mail truck and I climbed in. We were rather crowded on the seat, what with twenty or thirty small canvas mailbags piled between us. We chugged off in a general northerly direction through gentle rain that turned the trunks of the madrone trees to glistening copper. Shreds of misty clouds drifted upward along the tree-clad mountain slopes that closely hemmed us in on either side, bent on joining their companions in the gray, weeping sky.

Yet it was not a sad day. Dogwoods gleamed white in the forest. Wild roses and purple lilacs bloomed by the roadside. White azaleas and ferns draped the banks. Tiny waterfalls cascaded down the slopes, gurgled through pipes under the narrow one-way road, and went dashing on their way down the mountain. It was a beautiful day, with new charms appearing at every turn of the road—and there were plenty of turns as we followed the contours of the wild Siskiyou Mountains.

At long intervals I glimpsed the outline of a house back from the road, half hidden among crowding firs, oaks and maples. But more often the only visible signs of human habitation was a structure the size of a doghouse set on a pole by the side of the road. These were mail boxes. As we passed them with unslackened speed, Tom would throw a mail sack inside. I waited, filled with suspense, thinking each time that he would surely miss, but he never did. And no wonder. Tom told me he had been driving this route from Happy Camp to Willow Creek and back again every day except holidays and Sundays for fifteen years.

We passed through the Hoopa Indian Reservation, where the Indians are not required to stay and where as many whites as Indians live. Arriving at the little town of Hoopa, Tom drew up before the post office, took a sack of mail inside. That little chore done, Tom threw some more mail bags on the seat beside me and climbed in.

"Hungry?" he asked.

"I sure am."

"We'll stop at the Oaks Cafe," he said, jerking his thumb in the direction of a tiny restaurant bearing the simple sign, EATS. In another moment we were there. I clambered down and Tom pulled across the street to a gas station. Inside, I perched on a stool. A good-looking Hoopa Indian girl in a smart, crisp waitress' uniform brought me a hamburger and coffee. Tom came in, fitted his long legs under the counter, and ordered a hamburger, which he consumed in silence. Tom, I began to discover, did not indulge in idle chatter.

I finished before Tom did and climbed into the truck to wait for him. We left Hoopa and came to Weitchpec, where the beautiful Trinity River pours into the mighty Klamath. There we turned northeast and from then on were scarcely ever out of sight of that great stream. Once in a while we paused briefly at a little white-painted dry-goods box of a building labeled with the imposing sign, UNITED STATES POST OFFICE, standing in a niche carved out of the mountain and forest. Finally at Blue Nose Bridge we crossed the hurrying, tossing River and proceeded up its left bank.

Soon Tom stopped at the foot of the trail that led to my cabin, dimly visible in the trees fifty feet above us. He hopped off the truck and had my baggage out of the back in a jiffy. Then he politely pushed me out of his way, got back under the wheel, and disappeared around one of the innumerable curves.

I drew a deep breath of relief. The bottom of the canyon lay in deep shadow. Evening had come. I gazed at the mound of baggage and boxes that had to be carried up the steep trail to my shack and sobered up. I had been feeling pretty young and gay all day. Now I felt as old as Methuselah. There was work ahead and no one but me to do it.

Two

I LUGGED and shoved and pulled my boxes and suitcase up the trail as far as the bars that made a feeble barrier to my property. They formed a token barrier only, since there was no fence, and whoever wished to do so could walk around them. There I dropped wearily down on my box of garden supplies and took time to consider. It was already twilight and I must hurry if I was to get my luggage up to the cabin before dark.

In the waning light the cabin looked lonelier and smaller than I remembered it, and the rushing, talkative river, three hundred feet practically straight down from the other side of the road, sounded nearer and somehow threatening instead of companionable, as it had been when I was here before. But I had not been alone then.

The walls of the cabin's main room were made of five-inch poles extending vertically from ground to eaves, the cracks being chinked with inch-thick withes. As an afterthought—and probably years later—someone had added a narrow lean-to at one side. Split shakes formed its sides and sometime in the dim past that portion of the shack had been given a coat of white paint, now weatherworn to a dull gray.

The cabin huddled on an irregular flat place only a little

wider than itself, and perhaps a hundred feet long, that had been gouged out of the steep mountainside. One corner seemed to rest against the four-foot trunk of a towering red fir tree, while on the other side a huge white oak appeared about to fall on it from the top of a fifteen-foot embankment. Here, I thought with a sinking heart, I was going to live for a year—if I could stand it that long, which at the moment I very much doubted. What was I doing here, anyway, sitting on a box in the Klamath National Forest, far from electric lights, plumbing, inner-spring mattresses, lectures, theaters—in short, from San Francisco? I should have had my head examined . . . but it was definitely too late for that now. I had to make my way up a twisting trail for fully a hundred yards to my cabin, and it would take several trips to get myself moved in. I decided one trip was all I could make that evening. The waning light really started me going.

I opened the carton of groceries and scrambled in it for the food I would need that night—a loaf of bread, butter, a pound can of coffee. From my suitcase I took matches, soap, a towel, my flashlight, a candle, my trusty little Iver Johnson pistol, and a nightgown. Then I started up the trail with all the speed I could muster—which was far from being speedy, as I had to stop every few feet and puff. I am sure my trail is the steepest short trail in the Klamath. My young legs failed me. As for my heart, I couldn't keep it from beating too fast, nor my breathing apparatus from wheezing like a leaky bellows.

I was played out all over when I reached the cabin door. Fortunately, I remembered where I had left the key two years before, and reached for it under a mossy rock. Something slipped under my fingers—a sleeping lizard, maybe—but I found the rusty key and turned it in the flimsy lock. I opened the sagging door, dragged myself across the threshold into

the main room and threw myself into a decrepit wicker rocking chair.

I could see that the musty little cabin was about as I had
left it when my friend and I had, as a last chore in the shack,
rolled up our bedding and by dint of much pulling and hauling had dragged the unwieldy bundle up to the ceiling by a
wire and anchored it there. This was to outwit any marauding
wood rat that might take a notion to make off with it piece-
meal. Directly beneath the roll of bedding stood a rough bedstead with nothing on it but springs, these being naked to the
public eye. The floor was bare boards, strangely uneven
under my feet.

It took me a few minutes to realize that I was getting nowhere sitting in the rocking chair. Pull yourself together, old
gal, I thought. Unfasten that wire and get your bed in shape.
You're going to need it powerful quick.

I rose from the creaking chair and jerked the wire loose,
spread the mattress and blankets on the springs, and my bed
was made. I took a peep into the kitchen with my flashlight. It
looked the same, except for a festooning of spider webs. The
large, ornate and ancient cookstove—which my friend had
declared was a museum piece dating back to the sixties—was
rusty in spite of our having given it a coating of rancid lard.
The coffeepot was still upside-down on the rickety table,
placed that way to keep a curious mouse from crawling into
it and dying there. Frying pan face down. Thick white plates,
cups and saucers—knives, forks, and spoons stacked in a covered fruit jar. The sight of them suddenly stirred my appetite.
I hadn't eaten since that lone hamburger at Hoopa, and I was
famished.

I lighted my one candle. Instantly the world outside was
enveloped in what seemed like pitch blackness and the only
light in the great Klamath Forest gleamed softly in my little

cabin. I touched a match to the trash in the stove and flames went roaring up the chimney. That made me think of water. I took a quart jar that stood on one of the shelves and made a forced run to the water barrel, fifty feet away in the back yard. It was fed by a pipe from a spring that gushed out of the mountain far above.

I knew by the way I stumbled when I ran and the way my hand shook as I filled the jar with water that the blackness of the night was beginning to scare me. The feeling of being alone on that vast mountainside, no neighbor within hailing distance, was working on my nerves. I might scream, yell, shout. None to hear. Just an echo from the bluffs across the river to answer me.

I pulled myself up short. If you think of trifles like that, my good woman, you're going to get really scared. Make yourself some coffee and toast and get down to earth. Back in the kitchen, eating toast and drinking coffee, I studied the back door. The man who made it had thoughtlessly left off lock and key. A light board across it kept out inquisitive small animals. But what about a bear? Or a mountain lion? There were plenty of these beasts in the Klamath Forest. Wildcats, too, probably. It behooved me to construct some sort of barricade for my own protection.

I set the one kitchen chair upside-down against the door and hung kettles, coffee pot, frying pan and tin lids on it. One slight jar would set the whole contraption tumbling with a din that would be sure to wake me and scare away any trespasser. I locked the front door, laid the flashlight and my little Iver Johnson pistol on a box by my bedside, and crawled in.

I was too tired to sleep, so I decided it was a good time to think. A gentle night wind stirred the branches of the giant fir tree that towered over my cabin. Now and then a fir cone hit the roof, punctuating the whisperings of the night. The big gloomy Klamath River, a stone's throw from my cabin, rippled, gurgled, chanted, on its way to the ocean. I knew the night wind would blow itself off, but the River was there to stay forever, making weird music like some goblin radio of the mountains.

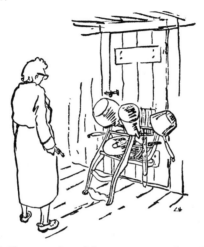

How blissfully comfortable it was to lie there, relaxed, thinking of the quiet hours I was going to enjoy in this, my new freedom— Good heavens! What was that? A sound like galloping horses right over my head! It can't be a horse, though, I thought. The attic isn't big enough for even part of a horse, and yet—a wild party of some kind was going on up there. Then came the unmistakable thumping of rats' tails. Rats are frightening things. *They've been known to chew people's ears when they were asleep*—or so I'd been told.

This was the time for desperate measures. I remembered seeing an old frayed broom in a corner of the kitchen. I made a dash for it—not without encountering a mouse that scampered across my bare foot. I screamed—or did I? It's funny about women people. We scream to be heard. Try screaming when you know the nearest human being is too far away to hear you. Seems sort of futile, and you wish you hadn't.

I jammed the end of the broom handle against the ceiling, the walls, the floor. I made night hideous for the visiting rodents. They got out and stayed out, as far as I know, for the rest of the night. I crawled into bed and attended strictly to the business of sleeping until next morning at daylight.

However, not daylight but starvation woke me. I lay thinking of my boxes and suitcase spending the night at the foot of the trail. A stray dog might have come up to the bars to investigate them and left his autograph. This tardy thought got me out of bed in a hurry. I lit the fire in the kitchen stove and started to dress.

I am not quick at dressing, and this morning a rap at my back door caught me barefooted, with my hair hanging down my back. Who on earth! I thought in consternation. The rap was followed by a jerk on the door knob and down tumbled pans, pots and kettles with a horrid din.

"Hello, in there!" called a man's voice. "We brought your baggage up from the bars. Anything the matter, Mrs. Patterson?"

I remembered the voice. It belonged to the young man to whom, two years before, I had left the responsibility of doing my assessment work. What on earth was he doing here at this hour of the morning? His cabin was five miles away . . . and what was his name? Though I had written him several business letters I could not remember . . . I'll just call him Dearsir until I find out . . . all this flashed through my mind in an instant.

"Nothing's the matter!" I called. "Just a minute." I hastily pulled on my shoes, screwed my hair into a bun, and opened the door.

"Dearsir, how nice to see you!" I greeted him, pleased as punch and shaking hands heartily. "But where did you come from?"

"Up the road about half a mile," he said. "At a place by the river we call Bent Pine Claim. My partner and I built a cabin there about six months ago, so as to be nearer our mine."

This was shattering news. So I was going to have neighbors. But no time to think of that now.

"Dearsir, tell me this—how did you know I was here?"

He got back at my little whimsey about his name with a chuckle.

"Dear Mad'm, when we went outside this morning we smelled smoke. To smell smoke in the Forest is to smell danger. My pardner and I looked all around, saw smoke rising from the vicinity of your cabin. We came down here on the run and found your baggage at the bars. And here we are to deliver it to you and to hope you're all right." He jerked his thumb at the young giant who suddenly appeared at his elbow. "This is my partner, Dear Mad'm."

"Pleased to meet you, Dear Mad'm," the tall young fellow said.

My eyes traveled from his boots up and up to the top of his head, and I saw he was handsome in a Norse god sort of way. I liked him at first glance.

"I'm pleased to meet you, Up'nUp," I said. We all laughed. It doesn't take much to make some people laugh. Youth—or just being alive at eighty—are enough.

"We pass this way every day, going to work up at the diggings," said Dearsir. "If you need anything, just holler. We'll fill your wood box now and carry in some water."

I shoved the pots and pans behind the door and made room for them to come into the kitchen, my dream of blissful solitude fading.

"Do have a cup of coffee," I urged, by way of showing my appreciation of their thoughtfulness, and with no idea they would accept.

"Don't mind if we do," Up'nUp said promptly. "Fact is, we started running up here before we'd set our coffeepot on."

I knew then that my company would expect something more than a cup of coffee and I had qualms, remembering the small supply of food I'd brought along. Reaching into my grocery box, I took out a loaf of bread, now minus the two slices I had eaten before I went to bed, and a half pound of butter that was supposed to last me a week. A good-sized jar of strawberry jam was tucked in beside the butter, but a mean little hunch made me overlook that. It was my one luxury. I laid six slices of bread on top of the stove and filled the coffeepot with water, enough for half a dozen men, I thought. While I was rummaging for cups in the cupboard and washing them, the bread burned—but only a little. Then the coffeepot boiled over and breakfast was ready.

Dearsir scraped the burn off the toast, Up'nUp buttered it with a heavy hand. When I saw my half-pound of butter melting away, I got rid of the mean feeling about the strawberry jam and set the jar on the table. Up'nUp's face beamed with hungry joy. I poured coffee and the boys attacked the food. I returned to the bedroom to comb my hair properly, then dragged the wicker rocking chair into the kitchen.

The six slices of toast had vanished and Up'nUp was getting into the second half of the strawberry jam.

"Maybe we're eating up all of Dear Mad'm's jell," Dearsir suggested, watching the wholehearted way with which Up'nUp dipped into the jar.

"There's more where that came from," I lied grandly, and laid my last twelve slices of bread on the stove. I knew it would take all of that to fill these hungry men and that the rest of my butter would melt into those slices like water into sand.

By this time I was ready for a little toast and coffee myself. I no longer cared about saving anything. In another moment I was in the race for toast and salvaged a slice. A few minutes later they decided it was time to go. Up'nUp cleaned out the

strawberry jam with a knife and licked it, his face shining
with bland satisfaction. I thought Dearsir looked worried at
the destruction to butter and jam and I said, to make him feel
at ease, "Come again and have breakfast with me. This has
been a real party."

What was bread and jam and butter compared to the good
fellowship of these friendly boys? There was no use trying to
fool myself about this—I had been taken possession of, willy-
nilly, and to some extent at least, my longed-for freedom had
gone a-glimmering.

They filled my wood box from a supply of stove wood somewhere in the back yard, found a pail and brought it in filled
with water.

"We'll be going to Happy Camp in the jalopy day after tomorrow," Dearsir said in parting. "If you should want to do
any shopping there, we'd be glad to take you along."

Then they were gone, striding up the trail toward their
mine.

Suddenly it occurred to me that I hadn't said anything
about my assessment work which mining law required should
be done by July 1. Oh, well, there had been no opportunity to
talk business, of course. I could ask him about it later. There
was plenty of time.

Three

AFTER Dearsir and Up'nUp had disappeared along the steep trail leading from my front yard to the placer claims, I went outside to take an appraising look at what I was pleased to call "my surroundings." In front of the cabin I found a spot about twenty by thirty feet that had been gouged out of the steep mountainside. Little attempt had been made at leveling it. A wonderful place to break a leg.

I seated myself on an oak stump that had been used for a chopping block and let my eyes drink in the sight of the tall firs and pines, the soft, cool gray of the early morning sky. The fringed limbs of the fir trees reached down welcoming arms and seemed to take me in their embrace. I knew I should be a woman of the forest. I felt myself sealed to this new strange way of living by bonds I could not see, but that made me one with God and his forest . . .

There was nothing to be done in the cabin that couldn't be put off. I sat there for an hour while the little grannyhatchets got used to the sight of me. I'm deathly afraid of lizards. but kept my seat, watching these small gray ones perched on rocks, pumping their funny bodies up and down, no doubt considering among themselves if I were a safe landing-spot for the jump game they were playing.

Then it occurred to me that I'd better look over my property back of the cabin. There was just room for me to walk between the huge fir that touched one corner of my cabin with its rough bark, and the steep slope that went plunging down to the road. On the other side of the shack there was still less room to walk between it and the bank that rose to a height of fifteen to eighteen feet. I chose the trail around the fir tree.

Once in the back yard, I saw a sagging wooden structure, half in, half out of the bank, which I later found out the boys called "the cellar." Apparently it was intended to serve as a place for storage and a cooler, but not a very safe one, I thought, as there were cracks in the door and roof wide enough for a squirrel or—horrendous thought—a skunk to squeeze through.

Further along the bank stood my water barrel, with its constantly replenished supply of cold, clear water. A few feet from the kitchen door was a weatherbeaten woodshed large enough to hold a month's supply of stove wood, even in the coldest weather. Next to the river side of my domain stood a half dozen small but thrifty peach trees, two apricot trees and a cherry tree that seemed to have lost much of its interest in life. The slender limbs of the peach trees were crowded with round green promises of future juicy goodness, but the apricot and cherry trees were not so prolific.

At the far end stood a roofless, six-foot-high light framework from which hung shredded remnants of canvas. This puzzled me for a moment. Then I saw it was what remained of an outdoor shower. Perhaps the boys would put this potential luxury in working order for me with a branch pipe from the one bringing water to my barrel. I could cover the framework with gunny sacks myself.

By this time the one slice of toast and half a cup of coffee that I had been able to salvage at breakfast began to feel like

a pretty slim meal. I went into the kitchen to investigate the
grocery box. I had underestimated the appetite of an octo-
genarian in the woods. It must be the mountain atmosphere,
I thought, that has pepped up my appetite. I took stock of my
groceries and was sure I had been a little hasty in my buying
at the store in Arcata. There remained barely enough on
which to eke out an existence for two or three days—provided
I had no guests. Well, fortunately, there was a grocery store
at Happy Camp and Dearsir had said he would take me there
day after tomorrow.

So I opened a small can of tomatoes with a rusty nail and a
stick of stovewood and devoured practically all the contents,
along with crackers and potato chips. I ate more than I
should, because I had my nose in a flower catalogue I had
picked up in Arcata, and nibbled potato chips as a sort of accompaniment to my rosy thoughts.

After my stylishly long time out for lunch I went back into
the bedroom to put on the poison-green garden hat and
flamingo-pink smock. Might as well start gardening right. As
I moved about I became conscious again of the strange unevenness underfoot that I had noticed the night before.
Stooping to look for the cause, I saw twelve-inch-wide floor
boards that were obviously hand-hewn. That meant, I knew,
that this part of my cabin had almost certainly been built
sometime before 1850, when the first sawmill had been
brought into this part of the Siskiyous—or so I'd been told.
This gave me a strong feeling of respect for my floor, but I
still didn't like the bareness and unevenness of it. Some kind of
rug would have to be devised—at least for beside my bed, but
I'd think about that later. Just now I was more interested in
getting my flower garden started than in rugs.

Out in the front yard I opened my box of bulbs and seeds.
The only digging implement I could find was a mattock, a
miner's castoff tool made for giants. I wouldn't let a thing like

that stop me, so I began hacking and digging until I got up a wonderful sweat that ran down my back and dripped off my nose. By dint of pitching rocks over the bank and beating clods with the mattock, I made quite a little headway in getting my ground into shape.

Among the many items I had bought for my garden was a box of chemical fertilizer which had a legend on the outside that ran something like this: "Excellent results without soil or sand. Only water is necessary."

Now I knew enough about gardening to see that I did not have either soil or sand—only partially decomposed granite. But my spring would furnish me lots of water. One must also have faith to grow flowers, and I had oodles of that. I dropped bulbs into the shallow trenches I had scooped out and covered them with granite—earth. Then, by means of a one-woman bucket brigade I watered them down with my chemical solution.

I had a backache by this time that made it impossible for me to straighten up, but I was happy. My flower garden was no longer only a dream, but at least the beginnings of reality. Looking around, I could see that each day, by using elbow grease and honest sweat, I could clear a bit of my little yard of rocks and trash, so that flowers might grow and bloom.

I had thought I might be lonesome just at first, but how could anyone be lonesome with dozens and dozens of lovely bulbs to sort and find out their names? Indeed, I completely forgot the boys and that they were coming by on their way to Bent Pine Claim after work. I was suddenly stricken with fear of what might happen. Those hungry boys would probably stop and expect to have supper with me. I could, of course, tell them the truth—that I had no food to spare—but I hated to have them find out I was so impractical—starting to live in the mountains without enough food to last at least a week. But the really forthright woman is as rare as a wingless angel and I was no exception. There was no use denying I was "up a stump," to use the vernacular. And how was I going to live in the backwoods of a great forest, far from the centers of culture, without using the vernacular, I'd like to know?

Then I heard them coming, yelling and shouting like twelve-year-old boys. I stepped briskly inside the cabin and closed the door, striving for time to think up a plausible lie that would explain my food shortage and still keep the respect of these new boy friends.

"Hi, there, you dumb brute!" Up'nUp shouted from somewhere up on the side of the mountain. "I'll break your neck when I catch up with you! Get away from that door!"

A terrific lunge against my kitchen door was the answer. I threw it open—and faced a mean-looking billy goat who plainly meant me no good. He tossed his shaggy head and greeted me with a vicious "Ba-a-a-h!" Back of him were a dozen or more glassy-eyed creatures who evidently made up his harem. I'd heard that billy goats butt on the slightest provocation, so I took no chances and slammed the door in his face.

Just then Up'nUp and Dearsir came down the trail in hot pursuit of their herd. Up'nUp, in the lead, gave a whoop that started the goats down my trail to the road. Dearsir paused an instant in his wild flight to shout at me, "We're taking the little nannies home! Bring you some milk in the morning!" And the whole entourage—men, nannies, and billy goat— were racing up the road in the direction of Bent Pine Claim.

Milk! I thought, dismayed. But I don't want any goat's milk!

One of my plans had been to lie abed of a morning until the spirit moved me to get up, but next morning I bethought me of those boys coming up with their goat's milk and most likely expecting to be asked for breakfast. So I rose at daylight, but with no plan of coping with the difficulty, if it arose. But I was spared. The men arrived early, puffing from their swift climb to my door.

Up'nUp carried a half-gallon glass jug full of goat's milk and a box of luscious-looking strawberries. Dearsir had a barley sack half full of something lumpy slung over his shoulder. He dropped it on the floor.

"We knew you'd be shy of fresh vegetables, so brought you some from our garden. There's about everything in that line you'll need for a few days." With that, he fumbled in the big pocket of his fishing jacket and pulled out what looked like a bundle of ferns. He opened it on the table. "I went fishing this morning and got a mess of trout." He spread them out—

sixteen big rainbows, cleaned, ready to pop into the frying pan.

"We see you've been planting a garden out front," said Up'nUp. "It isn't a likely spot for vegetables. Onion sets, for instance, need good loamy soil." He went on seriously, "That is, if you expect them to make onions."

"I wasn't expecting them to make onions," I said, very serious, too. "I have set out ixias and sparatis and scillas and—other things."

"Oh, well, I don't know much about these new-fangled vegetables. But Dear Mad'm, I think you need soil for any kind of vegetables."

"These are *flowers*," I protested vigorously. "And they don't require soil. I have a chemical that makes them grow in water."

"Oh, gosh, Dear Mad'm, you need something besides mineral water. You need—" I thought he was going to say "common sense." "Well, anyway," he went on, "you need fertilizer and I'll fetch you two sacks of goat manure tomorrow morning. It's sure-fire stuff."

Now, I thought, how will I ever know if it's goats or chemicals that make my flowers grow?

The boys refused my invitation to have coffee, much to my relief, but said they'd drop in for supper and help me eat the trout and strawberries. "Keep the milk in the cellar and the cream'll be fine with the berries," said Dearsir. He must have seen the expression on my face, for he added anxiously, "Don't you like goat's milk, Dear Mad'm?"

A white lie came to my lips. I couldn't offend these kind-hearted boys. "The truth is, I never use cream on berries. As for goat's milk, I've only tasted it once and I thought it had—um—a—an insipid flavor."

They looked at each other, and I thought Dearsir winked at Up'nUp. "You sound like some women we know here on the

River," he said. "They vow they can taste goat's milk in spice cake and are sick at their stomachs for a week if they find out they've eaten whipped goat's cream on strawberries. Now tell me honestly, did you smell our billy goat when we took him by here last night?"

"Oh, was that what I smelled?" I exclaimed incautiously. I didn't tell them I was almost nauseated by their billy goat. "Well, really, you know—I'm not used to billy goats and—and I might get used to the smell, you know—" I stammered through this lame apology, trying to be truthful as well as tactful and getting nowhere.

"Well," said Dearsir, "as long as you don't tell us you can smell him as he walks along the road half a mile away, we think you'll pass. A billy smells—you bet he smells—but we won't let him come your way again. We'll be taking him off to pasture in a few days. Until then we'll keep him staked out on the bar down by Bent Pine."

"The little nannies don't smell bad," put in Up'nUp, defending his pets. "They smell as sweet as babies."

All babies don't smell sweet, I thought, remembering a woman who believed it was "agin natur" to wash wet didies.

We had a square meal that evening. No bread or butter, of course, but everything else anyone could want. Rainbow trout, potatoes, green peas, lettuce, radishes, and green onions in a tossed salad, minus dressing, topped off with strawberries and cream—minus cream for me.

After supper the boys set several traps in a well-meant but, as it proved, a futile effort to rid the cabin of rats and mice. They got a lot of fun out of it. I tried not to jump when the horrid little traps went off with a snap when they weren't set just right. They laughed so uproariously at my involuntary jumping that I suspected them of considerable trickery. Afterwards I was glad that I did flinch and jump at every sharp snap. I am sure there would have been two disappointed boys if I had been the stolid sort. I exemplified their idea of feminine behavior and they liked something feminine, even though frayed and worn by age.

After they left, I went to bed feeling protected against rats, mice, and house-breakers. I had stacked up Contraption, improving its architecture and making it more devastating if it should be disturbed. This, I said to myself, is part of my secret life. My friends must never suspect me of such weakness and folly.

Four

━━━◆◆◆◆▶━━━

THE following day at my new home I did quite a bit of
walking. I covered the ground pretty well for a distance of fifty yards or so, re-examining the cellar with
the sagging door, the decrepit woodshed, the skeleton framework of the potential shower bath. The whereabouts of that
other building we've read so much about in recent literature
was a mystery and it seemed best to solve it without further
delay.

I saw a faint trail covered with dry pine needles leading up
a steep slope from my front door. It looked as if it had been
much used at some time in the past and so might be worth
investigating. After following it at peril of life and limb for a
hundred feet or so, I saw a tattered mail-order catalogue
sprawling among the needles. I'm on the right track, I
thought. That's an age-old signpost that'll lead me to the Spot.
Sure enough, there it was, not far away, open to the whole
world of fresh air and mountain vision, with a simplicity of
architecture that belongs to men in the open. A pole laid between two logs. And that was all.

Our beloved James Whitcomb Riley started us off on the
subject of outhouses. Then came the Specialist, and on down
the line to the present day. People have split their sides laugh-

ing over this subject, but personally I've always found it lacking in novelty and rather dull. It's the point of view, of course. Mine was a wide one on this particular day. It took in several adjacent mountains and a slice of distant Mt. Shasta. I had a deep sense of security and privacy that some people in recent fiction didn't seem to have. And thinking about it I got to chuckling to myself.

I carefully slipped and slid down the pine-needle path to the safety of my front door. There I told myself firmly that I'd have to go modern and ask the boys to put up some sort of framework on which I could hang sundry burlap bags. I had other notions, too, about a can full of ashes and a board or two. It would be crude, but I wouldn't have to travel that dangerous pine needle trail to reach it.

Next morning before I was fully dressed I heard a noise in my front yard and took a peep to see what was happening. It had already happened. Up'nUp had completely covered my front yard with rich black soil that was already sending out a strong goaty smell. I met him at the kitchen door. He gave me no time to speak about the ill-smelling goat manure, but pointed severely to several boards lying on the ground.

"We're pretty shy of lumber right now, Dear Mad'm," he said. "Been putting all we could rake and scrape up into building more flumes up at the diggings. But we made out with what we had—all but the door."

His face was set in a stern expression and his voice sounded savage, as if he wanted no conversation from me. "Nobody uses this trail but us and old Pete, so we thought you could manage till we got some more lumber."

Without waiting for me to make out these cryptic remarks, he bolted down the trail to the road. I went back into the kitchen and looked out the window. I saw Dearsir and Up'nUp toiling up the trail, bent under the weight of the

heavy boards on their shoulders. Up'nUp's right arm was
thrust through a large hole in the board he was carrying awk-
wardly before him.

Instantly I saw the whole setup. I closed the kitchen door
and remained discreetly inside the cabin, though I was aching
to be out there and lend a hand. They didn't know, or forgot,
that I was old enough to be their grandmother and that privies
and backhouses and bathhouses were all in the same category
to me and that I shouldn't mind them at all. But, I thought,
suddenly remembering something Up'nUp had said, *Who is
Pete?* No doubt a neighbor with delicate sensibilities, I con-
cluded.

The sound of hammering went on. I busied myself unpack-
ing the few clothes I had brought with me and hanging them
in the tiny closet. My thoughts went back to the problem of
food, now an acute one. Oh, well, the boys had promised to
take me to Happy Camp that afternoon. So all would be well.

I became interested in watching the antics of several brilliant yellow-and-black orioles outside my window and forgot
there was such a thing as time. Suddenly I became aware that

the sound of hammering had ceased. It was so quiet I knew the boys had left. They have probably gone up to the diggings, I thought. I'll go out and have a look-see.

There, about fifty yards away, in a little nook off the trail that led to the mine was the tiniest structure that a full-grown human being ever backed into—sans roof, sans door, but with a comfortable-looking seat. This last, I found out later, had been sandpapered and then rubbed to a satiny finish. The whole thing had evidently been worked out up at the boys' cabin and then quickly assembled on my premises. I call that a piece of thoughtful gallantry less romantic but far more practical than Raleigh's cloak-throwing for Elizabeth.

But the question kept recurring to me with nagging persistence—*Who is Pete?* Must be someone living fairly near, though I had seen no other cabin. And what business did this Pete person have using the trail to our placer claims? I'd ask the boys next time I saw them, feeling faintly annoyed. I'd come up here in search of solitude, only to find that this part of the Klamath Forest was becoming overpopulated and I didn't like it.

Noontime came and I ate my meager lunch. Despite my hunger, I couldn't bring myself to piece it out with goat's milk, though there was assuredly plenty of it.

Five minutes after I had finished eating, Dearsir stood at my back door.

"Get your bonnet, Dear Mad'm," he said. "Up'nUp and the jalopy are at the foot of the trail. We're going into Happy Camp for groceries, and also nails and lumber to replace the flume that washed out last week. I take it you have some shopping you'd like to do." His sharp eyes took in the fact that there was nothing edible on my table, except a few crumbs.

"Be right with you," I said, getting my coat and hat from the closet, and my purse, which had been replenished from

San Francisco. A few minutes later Dearsir and I were at the foot of my trail. There sat the jalopy, its nose headed north, Up'nUp at the wheel. I got in beside him. Dearsir sat on the back seat beside a small suitcase. I wondered briefly about this bit of luggage, but dismissed its presence with the thought that it wasn't important and none of my business, anyway. We chugged and rattled off along the narrow, twisting road high above the tumbling, racing waters of the Klamath. In a very few minutes we came to the boys' cabin, built on a flat piece of ground close to the river. Here was space for a large tool house, chicken house and run, a good-sized vegetable garden, and perhaps a dozen fruit trees, too young to bear yet.

"This is Bent Pine Claim," Dearsir said, restrained pride in his voice.

"It looks like a nice place," I enthused. "But why Bent Pine?"

"Because there are four pine trees—you can't see them from the road—that were almost washed away by some great flood many years ago. They are big trees now, but all their trunks are bent at about four feet from the ground. So we named the claim where the cabin stands Bent Pine."

By this time we were around another curve. The road was narrow, but there were fairly frequent turnouts and I could see at once that Up'nUp was a careful driver and knew every foot of the road. This seemed to be a good time for me to find out about my mining claim.

"It's only a little over two months until the First of July," I began. "Have you done my assessment work yet, Dearsir? I'm really anxious to see it done."

There was a moment of silence.

"Not yet," he said finally. "But there's no cause for anxiety. You can trust me to get it finished on time."

There seemed nothing more to say, so I kept quiet.

At that moment we rounded one of the hairpin curves and I saw a giant of a man striding along the brink of the road ahead of us. He was stripped to the waist and a huge bowie knife, unsheathed, dangled from his belt. In his right hand he held an open book which he appeared to be reading and in his other he grasped some small object from which he nibbled now and then. One misstep would have sent him plunging to his death on the rocks far below. As we neared this fearsome apparition he turned and waited for us. It was then that I saw his short gray beard, stiff as an old wolf's hackles, and a chest covered with coarse gray hair. He stopped reading, but continued to nibble at what I recognized with horror to be a bulb of garlic.

Up'nUp stopped the car. "Climb in," Dearsir invited from the back seat. "Dear Mad'm, this is Frenchy—lives down the Klamath a mile or so from you."

So this was the eccentric neighbor I'd heard about.

Frenchy climbed in and seated himself beside me.

"Bon jour, Madame," he said.

"Bon jour, M'sieur," I quavered, trying desperately to remember my rusty French.

The light of joy that blazed in his face was wonderful to see. He came back with a torrent of French that poured through his beard like water over a dam. I had almost no chance during the rest of the way to reveal my lack of skill in speaking his language. He was voluble. I bobbed my head and said "oui-oui" when he stopped for breath. Maybe it should have been "non-non," but all he needed for encouragement was an occasional mumble in his native tongue. But when one or other of the boys broke in with an enquiry as to how his vegetables were coming along, or what progress he was making on his claim, he spoke perfect English with an Oxford accent.

We crossed Clear Creek, leaving behind the tiny post office

there, and the two huge buildings that had once been a resort, but were now only empty shells. The old jalopy rumbled and rattled, but I was used to that by now. Besides, I had my mind on other things. There was Frenchy and his garlic on one side, and on the other, beyond Up'nUp, great clusters of pink azalea blossoms hanging from the sheer rock cliff, interspersed with lovely yellow flowers called Oregon Sunshine.

Suddenly, around a curve ahead came a great trailer truck hurtling down the grade toward us. Its load of enormous mining machinery towered high above the top of our puny jalopy. Up'nUp slammed on the brakes. I grabbed Frenchy's arm and pushed my feet hard against the floor boards. The lumbering behemoth slackened its speed. Up'nUp stopped, began to back the jalopy. Around one curve—around another . . . ah! a turnout! Room enough for that dreadful truck to pass. On it came. The driver waved nonchalantly as he rolled by.

"That wasn't bad," Up'nUp remarked, starting forward again.

"Now you take that time I met one of those mining trucks with most of a dredger on it—had to back a quarter of a mile."

You take it. I don't want any, I thought bitterly, straightening my hat and my nerves, both thrown completely out of kilter by what had happened. We traveled several miles before I calmed down sufficiently to notice once more the white, ethereal beauty of the dogwoods and the wealth of graceful ferns that bordered the many tiny streams foaming down the mountainside.

Finally we came to a stretch of road where the bank on our left rose sheer for thirty or forty feet, and above that the mountain shouldered abruptly into the sky. To my startled eyes the bank seemed to overhang the road, but my reason told me that would not have been done, even by the impossibly reckless engineers who had built this crazy road. On the right, only two feet beyond the wheels of our car, the ground plunged vertically to the river, two hundred feet below.

I must have done something—said something—but I have no idea what. Up'nUp glanced at me.

"Dear Mad'm," he said, "your face is plumb white. There's nothing the matter with this road. At least, not on a nice clear day like this. Now at night, when it's raining cats and dogs, and there's mud slides and rocks rolling down the mountain—"

"What are you trying to do?" Dearsir said, "scare Dear Mad'm to death?"

"Tut-tut, boy—let Madame enjoy the scenery," rumbled Frenchy.

"Scenery be damned!" Up'nUp spluttered, a little angry.

A mile or so farther on we drove into a lovely wooded valley, crossed a sparkling stream, and were in Happy Camp. I looked around, disappointed.

"Why—I was told this was an Indian village," I said. "Where are the Indians? Where are the tepees?"

The men laughed. They didn't even bother to answer me.

We drove down the main street of this straggling little village and parked in front of the one store. Beyond it was the Del Rio Picture Theater, holding forth in a remodeled store building and offering one show a week. We got out. I saw a few Indians, but they were singularly unexciting, because they wore the same sort of clothes, had the same kind of haircuts, as everyone else. Across the unpaved street a tall Hoopa Indian dispensed gasoline and oil at a service station.

We all went into the general store. I bought a sensible assortment of groceries, in sensible amounts, then drifted over to where there was a limited assortment of dry goods on a table. A feminine voice at my elbow said politely, "May I help you?"

Turning, I saw a pretty, neatly dressed Indian girl smiling at me. I smiled back.

"Why, yes," I said. "Have you any bleached flour sacks?"

She pointed to a stack of them lying on the counter.

"Six please," I said. "I'm going to make window curtains of them." Seeing her look of surprise, I added hastily, "I shall dye them, of course. Do you have any yellow or green dye?"

"I'm sorry—we don't have dyes of any kind."

"Oh, well," I said airily. "Doubtless I can manage. Boiled onion skins give a nice yellow. And green—well, I'll find something . . . Give me two spools of white thread, Number 50. That will be all."

The girl looked at me with what I hoped was respect for my versatility and knowledge in the matter of dyeing curtains, wrapped my package, and courteously told me goodbye.

At the back of the store I bought a hundred feet of garden hose and a brass faucet. This last item Dearsir had promised to put on the end of the pipe that brought water from the spring to my back yard. This, and the hose, would make it possible for me to water my flowers with practically no effort.

Meeting the men at the door, we went together to the car, stowing our purchases inside. Then we parted, Dearsir and Up'nUp declaring their intention of buying some lumber, if any could be found. Frenchy disappeared on whatever mysterious business had brought him to town. I went back to the store and gazed around at the various items in stock.

Soon tiring of this limited pastime, I followed a side street lined with simple but pretty homes, each with its flower garden rioting in color and perfume. In a sort of trance, I wandered on and on, turning this way and that, exclaiming to myself over the beauties I found everywhere. Jonquils, hyacinths, tulips, all the spring flowers I knew and some I didn't. Roses clambered up trellises, honeysuckle-garlanded fences. I loafed along, lost in the ecstasy of flower worship, unmindful of the passage of time. Suddenly I was at the last house, right on the bank of the river. There I was brought back to earth by a sharp, breathless voice unmistakably speaking to me.

"Well! So *here* you are! I hope you have enjoyed yourself, Dear Mad'm. We got the whole town looking for you."

It was, of course, Dearsir. The worry he had felt about me sharpened his voice. People peered out of doors and windows. Chastened, I climbed into the car, and we started off.

"Don't you feel bad, now," he said gently. "Suppose you'd fallen in the river, like we were afraid you'd done? You've given us a bad half hour. You can thank God, Dear Mad'm," he went on, "that the Happy Camp newspaper correspondent didn't find out what was going on, or you'd have made the headlines in tomorrow's *Siskiyou News*."

We came to the main street. To my surprise, Dearsir turned the car back the way we had come.

"Where's Frenchy?" I asked. "Where's Up'nUp? We can't go without them!"

"That's what we are going to do," he answered. "Frenchy came in to go to the picture show. He'll catch a ride back to-night—or he'll walk. Does it every week."

Walk eleven miles along that horrible road? I thought. Well, anyway, at night he wouldn't be reading a book as he went.

"But Up'nUp!" I persisted. "Where—what—"

"He had his bag with him—maybe you saw it on the back seat—and he took off for Yreka," Dearsir said, then closed his lips firmly. I knew I'd get no more information from him just then. He drove around curves, next to precipices, along that dreadful stretch with cliffs above and below, in silence. Only once, and that within a mile or two of home, did I manage to break his uncommunicative mood. That happened when I saw a suspension footbridge stretched across the canyon high above the Klamath River. It looked almost frail enough to be the work of an industrious spider. Near where its further end met the bank I glimpsed among the trees a large, well-built house—six or seven rooms, maybe.

"Dearsir, who on earth lives there?" I demanded urgently. "And how do they get the necessaries for living across that flimsy bridge?"

"Family by the name of Benning lives there. They're part Indian—not much, though. You'd never know it by looking at them, especially the children. As to how they get their stuff from this side of the river to their house, they carry it across that bridge, that's how. They have to leave their car on this side, of course."

"But—but—why don't they live on this side of the river?"

"There's no accounting for the foolishness of people, Dear Mad'm. I quit trying to do it years back."

There was silence again.

It was growing dusk as we arrived at Bent Pine and drove down the short roadway, past the tool house and stopped before the cabin. A beautiful little black-and-white shepherd dog ran to meet us, barking joyously.

"There now, there now, Vicki," Dearsir said, patting her slender head. "Hush, like a good dog." She stopped barking instantly, but her plumy tail continued to wave with abandon. We got out and went in.

"We're both hungry," he said. "I'll just heat up some grub and make coffee."

While he built a fire in the cookstove and went about preparing food, I sat down and looked about me. The room was orderly, clean and a trifle austere, as became a bachelors' abode. All except a huge cluster of wild azaleas on the table, their stems thrust into a mason jar. Half a dozen late magazines lay on a side table, book-filled shelves almost covered the wall.

A gun leaned in a corner by the books—a regular he-man gun. It terrified me, just to look at it.

"What kind of gun is that?" I asked.

"A 30/06 Enfield rifle. Not much like your little Iver Johnson, is it?"

"No—not much," I said. "Do you suppose I could shoot it?"

He laughed. "You'd have to lift it first. Then aim it and hold it steady while you pulled the trigger. It weighs over eight pounds and is about forty inches long. Think you could?"

"Yes—if I was frightened enough."

"Maybe so—maybe so," he said, in the voice of one humoring a child, and turned back to the stove.

My eyes traveled to the wall opposite me. A great brown bear hide was stretched on it, the very thing, I thought, to cover the rough planks of my bedroom floor—soft, woolly, warm to the feet. It served no useful purpose here—why not ask—I caught myself up short. What an idea! No, I certainly wouldn't ask the boys to give me their bear skin . . .

Dearsir caught me looking at the furry thing.

"Up'nUp shot it," he said. "Last winter—not far from the diggings. We'd seen its tracks."

"You mean there are *bears*—right around *here?*" I interrupted.

"Some," Dearsir replied calmly. "Other animals, too, such as bobcats, deer, a cougar once in a while. But they're even more afraid of us than we are of them, so don't worry. Up'nUp had to really hunt for this fellow. He likes to tan hides and he's right good at it, too."

"We-e-ll," I said uneasily.

"Now don't you give wild animals another thought, Dear Mad'm. Likely you'll never so much as see one."

He set the dishes of food on the bare table. Everything tasted wonderful. There were beans, of course, bacon, eggs, bread and canned purple plums. I did full justice to the fare.

Vicki climbed up on the bench beside me, leaned her head against my arm.

"It's all right," Dearsir said to my questioning look. "She never forgets her manners. That's as far as she'll go." I patted her shoulder, felt her press against me, quivering with joy.

Supper finished, our cups filled the second or third time with black, steaming coffee, Dearsir told me about Up'nUp. He was married, young Up'nUp was, to a pretty telephone operator in Yreka, a good-sized town some thirty-five miles easterly on the winding road leading from Happy Camp. He went on to comment on matrimony in general.

"That's one business it's absolutely safe to stay out of," he declared. "Looks like it's sure to bankrupt you, one way or another." Then he became more specific. "Take Up'nUp, now. He and his wife—Nora's her name—don't appear to get along at all. Yet he sends her money every time we clean up at the mine—and sometimes when we don't. Every once in a while a notion strikes him and nothing will do but he has to go see her. She's young and healthy—able to take care of herself, make her own living. What's the matter with the boy? Seems to me he acts plain unreasonable."

"I don't know," I said slowly. "You can't always tell about people. You don't always have to like someone in order to love him. Maybe he doesn't quite understand, himself—"

"I'm sure he doesn't," he interrupted me. "It's a mixed-up business, if you ask me. Well, you must be tired. I'll take you home now. Coming with us, Vicki?"

He drove me to the bottom of my trail and carried my packages up, put them on the kitchen table.

"Goodnight," he said. He and Vicki went out into the darkness. I undressed as quickly as possible and slipped between my soft cotton blankets. So much to do tomorrow, I thought. Sighing contentedly, I went to sleep.

Five

———◄••►———

THE days lengthened as summer drew near. Except for giving my swiftly growing plants plenty of water, I had almost nothing to do. Sometimes weeks passed when I saw no one except the boys passing by on their way to the mine, and occasionally Frenchy striding along the road, going to see a picture show at Happy Camp. If I were out in the garden he would shout a few words and go on. One of the nice things about Frenchy was that he never bothered anyone. He was always going somewhere, in too much of a hurry to stop for idle chit-chat.

So I had the long peaceful days of solitude which I had promised myself would be mine here in my little cabin home in the Klamath Forest; days to which I had looked forward with such eager longing. But after about the third such day in a row I got darned tired of them. There's something about people—oh, well, what human being was ever completely satisfied, completely happy, when he had achieved his dream? Human nature is a perverse and contrary thing—most of all, female human nature.

This particular afternoon I hadn't so much as seen a human being I knew for more than a week—just strangers now and then driving along the road; here one minute, gone the next. The boys, after making sure I had everything I would need until they returned, had gone to Arcata, a lumber town, to get boards for building flumes.

I sat slumped in the creaky old wicker rocking chair in my bedroom-sitting room, feeling very much alone. In the back of my mind a tiny thought keeps nagging at me. *San Francisco—at this very minute maybe the lovely damp fog is drifting in, turning the Golden Gate bridge to ghostly loveliness—and my friends—if I were there I could go to see any one of them . . .*

Stuff and nonsense! I am perfectly happy here! I told myself.

Resolutely I began to read the *Atlantic Monthly* that Tom had left in my mailbox early that morning. I should like to pose as an intellectual who never reads anything less literary than the *Atlantic Monthly,* but in the interest of truth I must add that Tom had also left me the *Siskiyou News* and *Life,* and I had read them both thoroughly before settling down to my old stand-by.

I was well into the second paragraph of a very interesting story when I heard the soft footsteps of a woman coming up the trail and felt a lively curiosity as to who it could be. When I heard a tap at my front door I opened it at once.

There stood a pretty girl—fourteen, maybe fifteen years old, I guessed. She was carrying a number of chrysanthemum plants loosely wrapped in a wet newspaper. She began speaking at once.

"I'm Milly Benning, Mrs. Patterson," she said, exactly as if she were speaking a piece at school. "I have come to welcome you to our neighborhood. I hope you will pardon my not having come sooner. My mother and I hope you will like it here on the Klamath."

So this was one of the Benning family that lived across the river at the far end of that narrow, frail-looking suspension bridge.

"Do come in," I said cordially, my admiration for the girl's wild-rose beauty blotting out for a moment my curiosity regarding her, my wonder at her fair skin, her light brown curls. I hastily brought in a chair from the kitchen.

She sat down, carefully arranging the pale blue folds of her pleated gingham skirt, placing her shiny black slippers together with precision, toes pointing straight ahead.

"I have brought you a gift which I hope will give you pleasure," she went on in an incredibly formal monotone, "some bronze chrysanthemum plants. I think neighbors should be neighborly, but without presum—" She paused as if she had lost her place, then found it again, in an invisible script she was reading, and went on, "I should say, without presuming on the relationship."

"Oh, you're right, quite right—I like to be neighborly, but as you say, without presuming." I was completely baffled by her composure, the stiff, rounded phrases that issued from her childish lips, innocent of artificial color. "Thank you so much for the chrysanthemums. I value them highly and shall plant them this evening after the sun goes down." I took the package into the kitchen, laid it on the table.

Now look here, I thought, considerably annoyed with myself, you go back in there and take control of the situation. It's getting completely out of hand. Are you going to allow that strange child to get you all flustered, make you talk like a character in a Victorian novel?

I returned to my guest.

"What a pretty dress—" I began, in an effort to get the conversation down to a more normal level. But I might as well have saved my breath.

"I hope you are enjoying our mild, salubrious climate." Milly's blue eyes were as expressionless as two lakes.

"Why, yes—yes, I am," I faltered, adding hurriedly, "Do you have a flower garden of your own?"

"Oh, yes. A garden helps to develop personality and should be a—an integral part of every woman's life. Don't you think so?"

"Well, I hadn't thought about that angle. I just like to grow flowers."

"Speaking of flowers," she went on, "perfume is very chick this year, especially flower scents. What is your favorite perfume, Mrs. Patterson?"

"Violet," I said, snatching at the first sweet-smelling flower that came into my mind. Milly looked disappointed.

"I thought it surely would be lavender—that is so suitable for aged persons. How old are you, Mrs. Patterson? Oh, dear!" she broke off in confusion. "I beg your pardon! I shouldn't have asked a personal question. Well-bred people abhor personalities."

This was more than I could take without making an effort to find out what was back of it all.

"I like personalities. Where on earth did you get the idea—"

"Why, from Emily Post's book." She sounded surprised at my ignorance.

"How did you come to have a copy?" I asked, realizing full well that I was indulging in personalities of the most flagrant kind.

"I saw it advertised in a magazine and asked my mother to give it to me for my sixteenth birthday. That was three months ago. I've been memorizing it."

"My word!" I leaned back in the old rocker, slightly faint at the idea of anyone memorizing Emily Post, admirable though the lady's written words undoubtedly are. I must confess I had never read her book—but then, one can't read everything. Why, I was way behind with my garden magazines.

"It *is* quite a task," Milly went on, "but I have heard that to be a lady you should know your Emily Post. And I *do* want to be a lady. But it's much easier to be just what you are."

So that was it. She'd been feeding me undiluted and undigested Emily Post. This child . . . now why on earth, I asked myself, do I want to laugh and cry at the same time? In an effort to cover up my conflicting emotions I asked the first question that came into my head.

"Where do you go to school, Milly?"

"Not anywhere at present. It's vacation now, you know. But when school is in session I attend the little country school at Clear Creek. Mr. Bond is our principal. He has only two pupils, a boy about my age and myself. He told me to study Roget's Thesaurus in order to improve my vocabulary. I've been working hard at that."

Emily Post's book and Roget's Thesaurus! Both fine books, but the combination . . . Milly's voice was going on.

". . . so next year we will both graduate, and after that there won't be a school at Clear Creek—unless some new people move in, and not many new people come to live on the Klamath."

For the first time she stopped reading from Emily Post and the Thesaurus. Her last sentence held a distinct note of wistfulness and her blue eyes looked troubled.

"Milly," I said, leaning toward her, "I'm so glad you came to see me. I get lonely, too . . ."

"Oh, Mrs. Patterson!" she cried, twisting her fingers together. "Do you, honestly? Sometimes I get so lonesome I could die!" Her feet shifted to a childishly awkward position, her slim shoulders drooped. I felt she was close to tears.

"I can see that you and I are going to be friends, Milly," I said with determined cheerfulness. "I can't get around much, but you can come to see me. After all, you live only about two miles up the road. That isn't far for a young girl like you."

"You—you're willing to be my friend?" Milly asked, sounding incredulous, almost frightened.

"Why, yes, of course. I'm old, it's true, and you may not want—"

"Oh, it isn't that, Mrs. Patterson! I don't think you're too old to be my friend. And I'd love—but—well—I must tell you something. My father and mother are both three-quarter 'breeds.' So you see—I'm really a Klamath—Indian." She drew a deep breath. "So," she went on, looking down at her tightly clasped hands, "maybe you won't want to—"

"Why, Milly Benning!" I exclaimed, the tortured thoughts of this pretty child clear to me at last. "I knew all the time that you were part Indian. And I can assure you, it makes no difference to me. You are a dear, lovely girl, and I shall feel proud to be your friend. It's no disgrace to be part Indian—or all Indian, for that matter. It's what you are that counts."

For one incredulous moment she looked at me. Then she sprang up, threw her arms around my neck and I felt her warm young lips pressed against my cheek.

"Oh, Mrs. Patterson! That's what Emily Post says—or something like it that means the same thing. But most people around here don't think that way! I want people to like me. I want so much to be polite and act like really nice people do. My father and mother—they're all right and they're very good to me, Mrs. Patterson, but they don't think things like that are really important. But I do. Would you show me how?"

"Why, yes, Milly, I'd be glad to. But really, all you have to do is just act natural—be your own sweet self."

She shook her head. "There's more to it than that," she said shrewdly. "I've tried, but I'm afraid I can't learn it from a book—not even Mrs. Post's book, though she's helped me a lot. Didn't I do everything right when I first came, Mrs. Patterson?"

"You did everything perfectly," I said hastily. "I was charmed." As indeed I was. My praise brought a quick smile

to her face. "You just keep on practicing and you'll do it more
—well, more easily."

She nodded. "Practice makes perfect, Mrs. Post says. And
she's right. You are too, of course," she added graciously.

Being bracketed with Emily Post gave me a slightly heady
feeling—something to live up to, as well. Now that Milly had
come out from behind her Emily Post and Roget's Thesaurus
façade and let me have a look at her as she really was, she
seemed older than she had at first. I realized how friendless,
even companionless, her life was here on this lonely stretch
of the Klamath River.

"There's one thing—a favor—I'd like to ask, Mrs. Patterson," Milly said hesitatingly.

"Yes? Go ahead," I encouraged her.

"Would you call me Millicent?"

"Why, yes, of course. But why, child?"

"Milly is such a common name. I've read several magazine
stories about girls named Millicent. I like it much better.
Milly sounds dark brown, but Millicent sounds pink." She
looked at me as if she were afraid that I might think it was
silly to think of names as having colors.

"What a nice idea," I assured her. "My name is Stella. What
color does that sound like?"

Her face fairly glowed at my approval. It was clear that
understanding of her imaginative ideas seldom came her way.
My heart went out to her as I realized that this was so.

"Stella sounds blue—blue like the sky," she said unhesitat-
ingly.

"Thank you, dear. That's the nicest thing that was ever said
to me."

"I really should go now." She rose. "I must get home before
my mother returns from Happy Camp."

"Doesn't she know you have come to see me?" I asked in
surprise.

"No, Mrs. Patterson." She looked down in embarrassment. Evidently she hadn't intended to tell me that. "You see—she would have said no. She doesn't like me to visit white people." I literally shrank at the word "white." This child's skin was the color of cream, many shades lighter than my own sun-browned cheeks.

Then another thought struck me—an unpleasant one.

"You mean she won't let you come to see me?"

"Oh, yes, she will now. I can tell her you invited me. That makes it all right."

"I see." Evidently her mother was disgruntled with the so-called white race—perhaps she had good cause to be—or on the other hand, she might be a too-avid reader of Emily Post . . . it didn't matter. I would see this pretty little girl again, and the thought was a happy one.

We walked outside.

"Goodbye, Mrs. Patterson," she said, and started down the trail.

"Goodbye—Millicent!" She turned and gave a wide and happy smile, waved her hand to me.

"Be seeing you!" she called. Which wasn't at all according to Emily Post, but very comforting to my heart. She liked me —I had broken through the dreadful shell she had built around herself—strictly for purposes of defense against a world she felt was hostile to her.

I went back to look at the 'mums she had brought me. They were fine plants and I decided to set them out in the back yard, along the path that led to the shower. I had spaded up the ground the day before and raked it smooth, so I would have no trouble getting them in before dark.

As I placed the last one, pressed the damp earth around its roots, I saw something that all but startled me out of my wits —the deep footprint of some wild animal in the soft, smooth earth in front of me. It was as large as the palm of my hand

and looked as if a great cat's paw had made it. I searched for
more, but could not find another one. No doubt there had
been many others, but I had destroyed them as I planted the
chrysanthemums. *What kind of animal had made that track?*

Scrambling to my feet in sudden panic, I ran into the
kitchen and slammed the door shut behind me. I confess to
feeling a real fear of the unknown that night. When darkness
came, I was afraid to light my lamp and went to bed by flashlight, after giving Contraption an extra load to carry.

Should I tell the boys? No, I decided I wouldn't. They'd
just laugh at me, call me a tenderfoot from the city. But I'd be
on the watch.

Six

———◆•••◆———

T HE next few days were full of small thrills and happenings unimportant to anyone except myself. I planted more flowers and began work on the two terraces, now in a state of disrepair, on the bank sloping steeply to the road. This involved work with the mattock, the carrying of rocks, and building retaining walls. I hadn't found time to dye curtains or write letters, even to my closest relatives and friends, but excused myself with the thought of the post cards I had mailed them from Arcata. At least they knew I hadn't gone into a state of coma or amnesia or something interesting like that. I slept long hours, lingered over my work with no thought of haste. But I knew that some day soon I was going to have to do something about those noisy rats that lived in the space between the ceiling and roof of my cabin. I would fill all the cracks in my cabin walls with homemade papier-mâché made of torn-up newspapers and flour paste, that's what I'd do. But not right away. I must first get my curtains dyed and hung at the windows.

Then there was the matter of a mysterious bell to occupy my mind and fill it with the wildest conjectures. I had heard it twice, once early in the morning when I wasn't dressed to go out and investigate, and once in the late afternoon when I was too tired—or too lazy—to do so. It had a clear, musical sound, quite unlike the coarse jangle of the bell that the lead nannie wore. Once the ringing came intermittently from far above the cabin on the mountain. The other time it seemed quite near, on the road below my flimsy bars. I promised myself to ask the boys about it the first time I saw them, but the days went by and I forgot to mention it.

Finally came a day when I could put off no longer doing something about making the inside of my cabin more livable, more attractive. The curtains came first, I decided. I had a large quantity of onion skins, most of them salvaged for me by Dearsir from the vegetable cupboard at the Bent Pine cabin, to tint all my flour sacks a soft yellow. But I wanted green curtains for my bedroom. What to do? Finally I hit on an idea, though I wasn't sure it would work.

I took the canvas sack in which Dearsir had brought me vegetables the second morning I was in my cabin, and set off down the road. Everywhere on the bank and along the little streams flowing down the mountain and along the road, there were quantities of small plants filled to bursting with the green juices of spring; wild spinach, water cress, and many others for which I knew no name. These I gathered in great lush handfuls, stuffing them into my sack. Back at the cabin, I first crushed these to a juicy pulp in a bucket, added a little water. Knowing that heat would change the delicate color, I swished and squeezed two flour sacks in this mixture. Then I wrung them as nearly dry as I could, flipped them smartly several times to dislodge bits of leaves and stems, and hung them out to dry. The resulting tint was a soft, faintly clouded green. Quite lovely and very artistic, I thought.

Dying the rest of the flour sacks was easier. I brought in a small wash tub from the cellar, set it on the stove. I then dumped in several gallons of water, all the onion skins I had, and the four remaining sacks. As this mixture boiled I punched and stirred it occasionally with the handle of my broom. When these flour sacks were dry their color was most satisfactory—a pale old-gold tint. Fringing them, tacking them up to the small window, was easy. Then I called it a day. The entire effect delighted me. The cabin suddenly became my home and I loved it dearly.

But as every homemaker knows, one thing leads to another. The curtains that improved the appearance of the kitchen so much, made the unpainted shelves, darkened with age, look worse than before. But I had no paint. So what to do? I solved the problem next day and quite simply, by mixing flour and water to the consistency of light cream and pouring in the contents of a small bottle of mercurochrome, thus producing as pretty a color as you'd wish to see. This covered the inside of the shelves nicely and brightened the kitchen, making it cheerful, even giving it a touch of gaiety.

Then, as a finishing touch to my bedroom, I put up a large *National Geographic* map of the world which I had found in the woodshed. The countries were in nice shades of blue, green, yellow, red, and violet. I tacked it on the wall facing the door, stood back and examined the effect with a critical eye. There was, I decided, a kind of unfinished look about it. That was soon changed by fitting carefully selected pieces of bark around it for a frame. The room really looked lived-in now.

The boys left goat's milk at my door every morning on their way to the mine, and an hour or so later I dumped it. I just couldn't make up my mind to drink it, or even use it in cooking. This would be one of my secrets. I had thought that when I got off by myself I would be an honest-spoken woman with the few people I met. But here was a predicament. I'd have to forego some of the truth—do a little make-believing. After all, this thing of being fearlessly frank at all times is not what it's cracked up to be. To like or not to like goat's milk isn't a life-and-death matter.

But goat's milk was not my greatest problem. The goats themselves were playing havoc with my nerves. They stood on the bank above my cabin and stared at me unblinkingly, turning their heads this way and that as I moved. They had a habit of gamboling on the roof of my cabin in the early morn-

ing. The first time I heard them I sprang out of bed, half asleep, thinking the shanty was being bombed. I ran into the kitchen, brushed Contraption aside, and threw open the door. I caught those little nannies and half a dozen kids in the act of leaping from my cabin roof to the woodshed and back in a game of tag.

I screamed at them and the little beasts jumped lightly to

the bank and scampered up the trail, almost upsetting my tiny outhouse. I made up my mind that I would tell the boys, in the strongest terms, that this was unbearable—that they must do something about it. Just then I heard Up'nUp come whistling up the trail.

"Hi, there, Dear Mad'm!" he called cheerfully. "Have the little nannies been around here this morning? We saw signs of them as we came up the trail. But you probably didn't hear them. They can pussyfoot by a sleeping dog without waking him. I'll see if they got in your spring again. They do that, sometimes."

Did I rail at him as I fully intended to do? No, I did not. And I was all smiles when Dearsir showed up a moment later. Women are like that—old women as well as young. But I was getting pretty tired of seeing twelve or more nannies standing on the bank above my cabin each morning, gazing at me with their pale, unblinking eyes as much as to say, "We think you are something queer and we're going to find out about you."

I always began by shooing them and ended by shouting at the top of my lungs. I tried throwing rocks and sticks, but the rocks never came anywhere near them and the sticks were always boomerangs. I've got that woman's way of throwing. I guess it's in the bony structure of the female of the species. But *I can handle a broom.*

One morning, seeing them standing in a solemn row watching me, I picked up the old, frayed specimen that came with the cabin and tore hotly out the door. Unholy rage took possession of me. I wanted to murder nanny goats—but most of all a billy goat. I couldn't see the billy but I knew he was tagging along behind the nannies in the brush. I was sorry to think the boys had lied to me about taking him away, but I had absolute proof that he was still with the nannies, and his evil presence was fast driving me to nausea. I ran toward the bank and waved and shook my broom frantically at the stolid nannies. I shouted. I screamed. Finally I swore.

"Curse you for a lot of horrid beasts!" I yelled. "Get away from here with your damned billy!" And when they got good and ready they moved on—not one second sooner.

The old nannie who was in the lead, the bell fastened to her neck jangling harshly, was as ugly a creature as God ever made. Coarse, dirty brown hair, long, pendulous black teats, a smudge of a tail stuck stiffly up in defiance of decency. Following her with dainty steps were the creamy white young mothers, not yet misshapen. And close behind, stepping prettily, light as fairies, glistening white and with faunlike shapes, came the kids.

"I think in time, if I see enough of those kids," I said to myself, "I might come to like them—the naughty little imps."

I found that the all-pervasive stench of the old billy began to get me down. I smelled it in the house—among my clothes. I sniffed suspiciously at everything I touched. I thought the smell was on my shoes—following me everywhere like a nauseous ghost. I said to myself, am I going to let this billy goat drive me crazy? Am I to be outwitted by a flock of shanty goats? I was flimflammed—utterly dispirited. I would have to ask the boys to remove their billy, or remove me. It was all very sad to think about.

After one of these wild hallooings I leaned against a fence post to catch my breath—but sprang away as if I had touched a snake. It was not a snake, but a coil of rope. It had a collar attached to it. Billy's stake rope! One of the men had hung it on the post, expecting to pick it up later as he passed. It was stronger of billy-goat smell than the billy himself.

I found a stick, plucked the horrid-smelling rope off the post and dragged it to the bank that overhung the road. There I dropped it and saw it lodge in the branches of an innocent wild lilac bush. Some day one of the boys would find it and say to his partner: "Just what I thought. You hung it on this lilac bush and forgot it."

The goaty smell disappeared from my premises. One morning when the nannies came to look me over, I decided to look them over, too. They were no longer afraid of me, so I got my hand on one of the little milk goats. In an instant the whole herd surrounded me—ten or fifteen of them. One little nannie reared on her hind legs and put her front feet on my shoulders. For a moment I was startled. Then I sniffed. Up'nUp was right. She was sweet—sweet as the cleanest baby.

I went back to the cellar and poured myself a glassful of cold, creamy milk. I laid all prejudice aside and found the milk delicious—as good as any Jersey cow ever produced. No use mentioning this to the boys, I thought. They may as well think I've always liked goat's milk.

By the second week in May my bulbs were pushing their green leaves through the earth of the front yard. The low retaining walls of the terraces rose slowly—it's hard work carrying rocks and fitting them in place—and I planted more and more flowers on the level spaces. The boys had been planning to help me in my garden, but so far there had been no time. They were trying to run all the gravel they could through the sluice boxes, as the law forbade miners to pollute the Klamath with placer tailings between July 1 and November 30. The time when they would have to suspend the washing of gravel was only about six weeks away. During the summer and fall the salmon and steelhead came up the river to spawn, and the clouding of the river with tailings meant death to them. During those months miners built new flumes, repaired their old ones, and made all necessary preparations for resuming the washing of gravel in the late fall.

One day as I was working in my garden old Frenchy hailed me from the road below. I don't know why I call him old—he was only seventy. The boys had told me he was a citizen of the United States and drew a pension, so he didn't have to work, but panned gold on his claim when and if he felt like it. They went on to say that he was always generous with his help to people living on the River.

Suddenly it occurred me that maybe I could make a dicker with him to help me by doing some of the heavy work in my garden. So I beckoned to him. He came up, book in one hand, garlic bulb in the other, and sat down on a rock. I told him about the man-shortage I was experiencing and asked if he would be willing to exchange a little work in my garden for subscriptions to some magazines I thought he might enjoy. How he must have laughed up his torn old sleeve—he was wearing a jacket that day.

He waved the garlic bulb in a gallant gesture and replied most respectfully, "Non, non, Madame, thank you very much —but the magazines, do not trouble yourself about them. I myself, Madame, subscribe to the *Saturday Evening Post, Collier's, Time, Coronet, Atlantic Monthly, Reader's Digest.* And of course, a number of lesser publications which I do not care to mention."

Such as, I thought, the Police Gazette and the like.

"I spend one-fourth of my pension for reading matter," he went on, "one-fourth to keep my body from starving—I grow a garden and fish in the river, of course—one-fourth I send to my relatives in France to keep them from starving, and one-fourth for Defense Bonds to keep my government from starving." He laughed heartily. I joined him. "But Madame," he continued, "it would please me extremely to help you in your garden without compensation."

Suddenly I saw this great, long-striding man working in my small garden plots among my delicate plants and knew my idea had not been a happy one.

"You are most kind," I said, careful not to hurt his feelings.

"Sometime I shall be happy to have you come and help me with my garden. I will let you know."

"At your pleasure, Madame," he replied, with what I felt sure was perfect understanding.

"By the way," I said grasping at the first idea that came into my mind in order to change the subject, "tell me, Frenchy, who is Pete?"

"Pete? I regret that I don't know anyone by the name of Pete. Does he live on the River?"

"Oh, yes," I returned confidently. "Up'nUp said he sometimes comes and goes on the trail leading up the mountain right here by my cabin, so he can't live far away."

"Strange." Frenchy shook his head. "Perhaps he is known to me by another name. But no one, except our friends, the boys, lives within miles of Bent Pine, your cabin, and mine."

"Well, no matter. But the boys have been so mysterious about him that I just wondered. How long have you lived here on the Klamath, Frenchy?"

"Many years—more than I care to remember . . ." And Frenchy was off on the story of his life. He told me a lot about himself that afternoon. He had studied at the Beaux Arts—his pictures were exhibited in a spring Salon. He had a photograph of one picture—proved it by taking it from his knapsack. It was the portrait of a young French girl. He spoke of her in a lowered voice, slowly and with dignity.

"She was my fiancee . . . I, a poor young artist . . . we were much in love . . . but we had to wait. She died. Then I joined the Legionnaires and went to Africa. No rest there . . . no peace anywhere. From there I traveled to many countries, saw many places, seeking—what? Finally I came to the Klamath River. Here I find a measure of rest beside this mighty stream. Here I hope to die."

The shadows were climbing the mountain slopes across

the River when Frenchy rose to go. I knew I would see him again. He had strange ways, ate strange foods, I was told. The people of the River did not understand his customs regarding eating and drinking. His language was strange to them, even when he spoke English. He was too odorous. Only real friendship and understanding can thrive in a garlic atmosphere.

Seven

————◆•••▶————

THERE were still azaleas and wild iris blooming in the
forest as May came to a close, and even now and then
I found the strange, exotic coral root that resembled
a cactus, but bore no thorns. There were a few tight green
buds on my pansies, that promised glorious color to come, but
no blossoms had yet appeared in my garden, though all the
plants looked fresh and were growing fast.

One morning, still in bed, I heard again that clear, insistent
bell. I pulled on my old red sweater and drew it close across
my chest for protection against the chilly morning air, opened
the window and listened. I tried to locate the direction the
sound came from, but failed and it quickly died away in the
distance. Later, I hailed the boys as they went by on their
way to work.

"Up'nUp, what's this bell I hear? It's not the old brown
nanny's bell. What is it?"

"Why, it's—"

"That must be the river bell you're hearing," Dearsir interrupted. "The river chants, gurgles, rings bells and beats
drums. Especially when it's high, as it is now, and the boulders are rolling."

Up'nUp looked astonished, but made no further attempt to
answer my question.

Dearsir's explanation of the bell didn't satisfy me. Next morning shortly after daybreak the bell woke me from a sound sleep. I crept out of my warm bed, cautiously moved Contraption, and quietly opened the kitchen door. I wanted to listen carefully to that bell and decide for myself whether it was rung by a spirit, a human being, or the waters of the Klamath River rolling boulders.

I listened intently. The sound had a wicked jangle to it, as if motivated by something of this earth with maybe a small brain attachment.

Then I heard the bell again—and saw what was ringing it.

The bell was rung, jangled or clattered by a creature with its head in my tiny outhouse. Two-thirds of the animal protruded in the cold morning air. But its head was comfortably housed in what pleased the creature to use as a stall.

Now I am acquainted with the rear end of several quadrupeds. Cows are unmistakable. Horses I recognize with no trouble at all. And so on, and on, and on. This creature had an appendage that looked like a short length of rubber hose with a brush attached to the end of it.

I stepped back cautiously inside the door and closed it. The bell went on with an occasional jangle, as if the owner had been disturbed by a gadfly or a wandering yellow jacket. I was in nervous haste for fear the creature would back out of my outhouse before I could act.

Then I opened the door again. I carried my Iver Johnson in my right hand for protection and used my left to gather rocks. I threw my first rock too hastily, without taking careful aim. It went astray in the brush. I ventured a little farther from the cabin, took better aim, and hit the mark.

That is, I hit the rump of the creature who had taken possession of my private premises. The animal didn't move an inch. But it let out an ungodly bawl. Some people might call it a bray. That is a weak word for the most horrible noise I ever heard.

The racket was made by a mule, I told myself. A mule that must be wearing a bell strapped to his neck. But why? For what reason? I tried my luck with another rock. This time the mule, big, black, and offensive, withdrew his head from my outhouse and bared his ugly yellow teeth at me. Uttering a prolonged hee-ha-a-a-w, he leaped down the bank and into my back yard.

My back yard wasn't large enough for a big black mule and myself at the same time. I gave way to the mule. Inside the kitchen, with the door well barred, I took a deep breath and considered the situation. I still clutched my Iver Johnson.

But one doesn't shoot mules, I reminded myself. I must use other, more subtle means to get rid of the brute. I must outwit him with a little brain work. I had been told that mules were very smart. Could it be that I had met my match, that the mule would win out? In that event, I would be a prisoner to a mule until help happened along in the persons of the boys, or Frenchy.

I heard the creature hoofing it about my back yard and I realized what would happen to sundry boxes of young seedlings I had set out there in the sun. Nothing but love of my flowers would have tempted me to open my back door.

The mule stood thirty, maybe forty, feet away. Stood with both front feet in my box of seedling petunias. Between us lay my garden hose, nozzle ready for action. With my temper flaring to white heat, I grabbed the nozzle, opened it wide and aimed a heavy stream of water right into the big hairy ear nearest me.

It worked a miracle. The big brute made a mighty lunge that carried him out of my back yard and up on the steep bank above it. It was a frightening prospect, having that huge creature up there, on a level with the frail roof of my little cabin.

He stood there for several minutes with an attentive look— I might say in his ears—as if he were planning further mischief to annoy and frighten me. He knew he had gotten himself up on that steep bank and that he would have to get himself down from there. I was anxious to know how he was going to do it. Jump into my cabin? Jump over my cabin? Or just act mulish and stay where he was? Balk, in other words. Spend the day with me.

At last he came to a decision, sidled briefly along the bank, and landed in my tiny front yard. I ran through the cabin, looked out my bedroom window. There he was, right in the middle of a bed of baby blue-eyes. A mule in a bed of baby blue-eyes is a heartbreaking sight. I had to think quickly or the mule would outwit me again, as he had four times before: first, when he bolted from my outhouse; second, when he bolted into my back yard; third, when he bolted up the bank; fourth, when he bolted into my bed of baby blue-eyes. Something had to be done—and quickly—to save my garden from further destruction.

That hundred feet of synthetic rubber hose still sprawled in my back yard. For the time being I had forgotten my young legs. Here, I thought, is where legs are more important than brains. At my command, they carried me in a stumbling run to the back yard. I opened the faucet wide, grabbed the hose by the nozzle and started dragging it through the cabin to the front door.

As I said before, mules are smart. Smarter than horses or dogs—much smarter than some women. Maybe smarter than some men. What I am sure of is that this mule was the smartest mule *I* ever heard of. He heard me coming with the hose. Of course, I was making a racket dragging it across the cabin floor, stumbling, whacking the nozzle against table legs, chairs, bedstead. This smart mule knew what it was all about and took no chances on being hit in the ear a second time.

I heard a lunge over the low garden wall . . . a second lunge to the little terrace below where my beautiful Madonna lily plants were just poking their first leaves through the earth. Then came a noisy scattering of gravel on the trail that led to the road . . . a rattle and a bang as a heavy body smashed over the bars. Clatter-clatter, thuddity-thud—down the road. All the while I was shutting off the water and running to the kitchen window—a matter of eight or ten seconds, I should say.

The big brute of a mule had taken short leave of my premises. It was safe now for me to go out and estimate the damage he had done. The baby blue-eyes were trampled into the earth. Great holes in the soft earth gave my pansy bed the look of a shell-pocked battefield. My Madonna lily plants lay crushed and broken. My anger flooded away in tears.

Hours later, I was still working, trying to salvage some of my battered flowers when I heard an unusual sound on the road below me. I laid my trowel down and crawled to the edge of the bank to see what was causing the rumpus.

Dearsir, riding a mule without saddle or bridle, guiding it with a long green willow branch! The mule, now at my bars, balking at turning up my trail! There was a pop of the willow branch on the mule's flank and another pop across his head. The mule made a sudden lunge up and over, smashing the bars to the ground. Dearsir seemed not the least upset by the mule's leap. He sat that brute as if he were master of the situation. The mule evidently thought so, too, for he brayed—not defiantly, but dolefully.

I had never before seen Dearsir up on anything taller than a saw-horse and I was truly astonished. He was so sure of himself—so jaunty on that big, raw-boned mule, so entirely at his ease. I laughed—loudly. But I quickly sobered when I saw

Dearsir's face. He was very angry and his voice was fierce when he spoke to me.

"Some blankety-blank idiot drove my mule off the range!" he shouted. "Up'nUp and I have been looking for him for a week. Here I find him on the road miles from home as we were coming back from Orleans. He's all tuckered out. Covered with lather—running as if the devil was on his tail!"

I scrambled to my feet, scared and stammering.

"Oh, that was terrible—I mean, that was fortunate—that you found him, I mean." I was feeling pretty guilty just then, and a little scared, too. Dearsir was *so* angry!

"This is the most useful mule in Siskiyou County," Dearsir raged on. "He packed all our pipe up from the road to the mine. He ploughed the ground at Bent Pine for our garden. He can plough anything."

Oh, could he indeed. Didn't I know.

"He is more valuable than any two horses in the country." Dearsir wiped the sweat from his brow and railed on. "This is the first time he has ever left his range and wandered onto the road. He didn't do it voluntarily. He has been frightened or driven off. I'd like to get my hands on the devil who did this to our gentle old mule."

He had convinced me that it wouldn't be pleasant for that devil.

"I'll take the old fellow back on his range. He has never bothered or disturbed anyone in his whole life. I'll lead him past your cabin, Dear Mad'm. He seems a bit nervous. I've never seen him skittish like this before. Quiet down, now! Nothing's going to harm you here. You're among friends, Pete, old fellow."

"Pete!" I screamed. "Did you call him Pete?"

"Sure—what else? That's his name. There, there, Pete. The lady won't hurt you. S'long, Dear Mad'm."

I sat on my doorstep and meditated. At last the mystery of

the identity of Pete was solved, along with the unaccountable sound of a bell. Only as long as Pete doesn't betray me—and smart mule that he is, he may do it—I'll continue to be Dear Mad'm to the boys.

Eight

AS THE weeks went by, gradually the retaining walls were finished and young plants flourished on the level bits of ground they provided. Honeysuckle, petunias, stocks and pansies, all the lovely blossoms of early summer, made a Persian carpet of both my back and front yards. A red climbing rose reached eagerly up the rough bark of the fir tree at the corner of my cabin. Tight green buds appeared. Soon they would unfold—I hoped—into the lovely roses that had been pictured on the box in which it came. I had very little irrigating to do—frequent gentle rains lasting for only an hour or two had taken care of that chore for me. Everything was wonderful. Of course I would stay out the full year, the time I had set for myself to remain in these idyllic surroundings.

One morning right after breakfast I determined to spend the day writing letters to friends. I assembled paper, pen and ink. I sat down at the kitchen table. I hadn't gotten very far when I heard the boys' jalopy stop with a rattle and a bang on the road below me. Dearsir came running up the trail leading Vicki, his beautiful little English shepherd dog.

"We're going to a mill near Arcata to get some lumber, Dear Mad'm. Be gone several days. I'm leaving Vicki with you for your protection."

"How nice!" I said, holding out my arms to the beautiful creature. But she turned an imploring look on Dearsir and ignored me.

"Don't mind if she isn't friendly at first. She's not a one-man dog and in a day or two she will love you as much as she does me. Maybe more. I'm giving her to you for keeps—that is, as long as you are on the River. You need a real protector—living alone up here as you do."

"Thank you, Dearsir. That's kind and thoughtful of you." While I spoke, thoughts raced through my mind. The boys were going away—even though only for a few days. *What about my assessment work?* I'd have to screw up my courage and ask.

"Just a minute," I said. "I am concerned about the legal status of my claim. Today's the second of June and I—"

"Don't you worry your head one minute about that," he interrupted me. "Everything will be all right. If it isn't too much trouble, would you go up to Bent Pine once or twice to see if the chickens are all right? We've turned the kids out with the nannies. They'll take care of themselves for a few days. S'long. We'll be seeing you." He gave me the end of Vicki's rope and went down the trail at a lively pace, leaving me feeling a little indignant. Now why, I thought, won't he talk to me about my assessment work? Why does he have to be so mysterious?

Just then Vicki tugged at the rope and howled plaintively. I pulled her into the kitchen and closed the door. I had heard a good deal about Vicki from the boys and seen her several times; first, the night Dearsir and I had stopped at Bent Pine and eaten supper there and later as she accompanied the men up the trail to the mine, which she sometimes did. But I had never really tried to get acquainted with her. Now I set about doing just that. I ran my hands through her silky hair, gently scratched her velvety ears and talked to her as if we were already in love with each other. After a bit, Vicki put her forelegs on my knees and laid her head on my breast, looking at me with her big intelligent eyes. I understood her. She was saying in dog language, "I love you. Be good to me and I will be faithful."

I went back to my letter writing, with Vicki's head resting on my foot. After an hour or so I opened the cabin door, but Vicki showed no disposition to go out. She continued to lie on the floor, her luminous brown eyes following me as I moved about.

"Vicki," I said to her, "you know what I need. Something to love me that asks no questions, that doesn't know or care if I am old or young, good-natured or ill-tempered, well-dressed or slovenly, sad or gay, but just me, an old woman who wants to be loved for what she is—right now."

I think Vicki read my thoughts, in her dog's way. She came close to me and licked my hand. From that time on we were understanding friends.

The afternoon wore away. It grew dark early. My letters finished at last, I went to the door and looked out. Black clouds tumbled and raced across the sky; the wind sighed fitfully through the forest that surrounded me. There came a low grumbling from the distant peaks. Vicki heard it, too, and roused herself, growled a protest. She knows what that grumbling's about, I thought, and she doesn't like it. I don't like it, either. I'd better get these letters down to the mail box before rain starts falling in earnest.

I hastily stamped the letters and put them in my little waterproof mailbag. We made our way down the trail to my doghouse-sized mail box, where I hung the bag with a clothes-pin so Tom could snatch it off without stopping the truck as he went by in the early morning. We hastened back to the cabin, and I lighted a lamp and prepared a quick supper for Vicki and me. Before we had finished eating, thunder was reverberating from the canyon walls with horrid, broken

rhythm, and intermittently flashing its anger at us. Vicki stood
it as long as she could, then ran, belly-low, across the cabin ·
and dived under my bed.

I tried to keep my courage up, but my thoughts would return to the story Dearsir had told me about a man who lived
in Happy Camp whose cabin was built under a tall tree. In a
recent thunderstorm lightning had struck the tree, jumped
from tree to cabin and gutted it, leaving the man homeless
and half-dead from shock. Not a pleasant thought when I
knew that my own cabin was not only under, but actually
leaned against a fir tree over two hundred feet tall. Why anyone in his right mind should build a cabin so close to a big
tree would be known only to the old miner who did it. I hadn't
given the tree much thought, but now, with the thunder
sounding closer every minute, I went out to have a look at it.

In the deepening twilight the lightning seemed even more
terrifying. I never did pose as enjoying a thunderstorm like
some people I know. I've always felt about thunderstorms as
Vicki does. I couldn't dive under my bed, because sliding
under beds has never been one of my accomplishments.

I determined to count between the flashes and the following roll of thunder. At first I could count twenty. Nothing to
be scared of yet, I assured myself. And about my tree—it had
stood in this spot on the mountainside for generations, un-
harmed. A grand, friendly tree, to be trusted. Why should it
turn traitor to humankind tonight, just because I happened
to be living under it? I tried this form of reasoning with myself, but it didn't work. It's hard to pin yourself down to reason when another part of you is in abject terror.

I ducked back into the cabin, pulled a shawl over my head
to shut out the blinding flashes, but I soon found out that
lightning has a way of penetrating your eyelids in a way no
mere shawl can stop. Then came the blinding flash my nerves
were preparing me for. The flash and the crash that was like

the falling of a million tin pans, all the same instant. The echoing reverberations were deafening. I grabbed a canvas cover off a chair, flung the door open, and plunged down the trail to a sheltered nook under the hill. There I cowered close to the ground. Vicki crowded against me, shaking with fear. I put my arms around her and pulled her under the canvas with me. Another blinding flash directly overhead and Vicki and I slid down on our bellies and hugged the earth while the terrifying din of thunder split the echoes in the canyon.

And then came the rain—big, heavy drops. A few seconds later, the pelting downfall wet me to the skin. I lifted a corner of the canvas and saw that across the canyon my beautiful mountain prospect was lighted with several blazing trees that stood like giant torches. I counted six of these fires—then covered my head with the soggy canvas to lie prone on the ground while Vicki licked my face in an agony of fright.

I had forgotten to pray. I hadn't called on God to protect me in my craven fear. Soon I knew the worst was over, because the thunder grew less powerful, the flashes farther apart. In some unorthodox way I had become conscious of God's presence. I knew that if He had wanted me, he could have let the lightning take me. Something like comfort and peace pervaded my soul. I dragged myself up from the ground and Vicki and I, clinging close together, dribbled up the muddy, slippery trail to the cabin.

Fir cones were falling thick and fast on the roof. The rain pelted it like falling bullets. I pulled off my wet clothes and crept into my warm, dry bed. Vicki gave one final lick on my hand and crawled under the bed.

Dear God, it's over, I thought prayerfully. Dear, dear God!

But in spite of all the nervous strain and emotional exhaustion, I couldn't sleep. Maybe it was because the rats in the attic and the mice that scampered over my floor every night gathered in greater numbers than ever before and held high carnival. The boys' traps had done no good—no good at all in ridding me of the pests. I myself would take measures against the four-footed fiends. When next morning dawned, I would stir up a large batch of shredded newspapers and flour paste. With this homemade papier-mâché I would stuff every crack in my cabin—that would fix them, I thought savagely, listening to them scurry, squeak, and chatter.

Toward morning I fell asleep.

Next morning broke clear and golden. No sound of rats or mice. I hoped they had gone out into the forest, because today I was going to do something that would result to the disadvantage of any who remained. They would starve to death, that's what. Then I remembered the chickens at Bent Pine Claim that I was supposed to feed today. My murderous intentions toward the rodents who were joint tenants of my cabin would have to wait. But not for long. Maybe I could find some old newspapers at the boys' cabin. If so, I'd bring them home with me and—Vicki licked my hand. I took the hint and got up.

After breakfast, I inspected the garden; front, back and terraces. My flowers had come through the storm very well. Most of them had lifted their faces from the mud into which they had been pelted by the heavy rain. They looked fresh and happy, with their heads bowing, turning this way and that in the soft breeze. Then I prepared to go up the road to look after the chickens at Bent Pine. I was in honor bound to keep my promise to do so, though I didn't particularly care for the half-mile walk along the road. I fully sensed that I was very much alone in that part of the Klamath Forest so I put my little Iver Johnson into a handbag and started off, Vicki running ahead, waving her tail happily. I followed her down the trail.

When Vicki reached the bars she stopped suddenly, stood

motionless for a moment, then started to move off into the underbrush, making a low growling sound. I reached the bars and looked down. The earth was soft from the night's rain— and there, clear and sharp, were several tracks such as the one I had seen in my back yard when planting Millicent's chrysanthemums; big round tracks with no marks of toenails, so no dog had made them. What, then? I hadn't the faintest idea.

Vicki came back, still growling, as if she hated to give up but knew her duty was to stay with me. I had an almost overpowering impulse to run back up the trail, lock myself and Vicki in the cabin. But that wouldn't do. I had a duty to perform at Bent Pine and no mere tracks were going to stop me. I dismissed my fright and set off up the road, resolutely thinking of other things.

As I hurried along I was in danger from getting cross-eyed with trying to keep one eye on the curving, narrow road and the other eye on the overhanging wild lilacs that grew on the bank and reached out long branches of misty flowers that tempted my thoughts away from temporal things, such as hungry chickens. I had never before seen such a living curtain of feathery blossoms. Most of the blooms were white or blue, but sometimes there was a great cluster that were shell pink.

Vicki slipped through the gate at Bent Pine, I shut it behind us, and we walked down the short road to the cabin. On one side of the road I saw a spacious tool house that I had seen only dimly in the darkness on my previous visit here. I stopped in amazement. Now I am no stickler for meticulous neatness—quite the contrary—but the astonishing disorder of this place shocked me. Most of the floor was covered with cartons holding old boots, ragged scraps of blankets, odd-looking pieces of rusty iron whose uses were unknown to me, and other mysterious objects. On a black, oily workbench lay a confusion of small tools, pieces of pipe, bolts, nails, screws, and so on—a complete inventory was impossible—piled to the depth of six inches in places. My fingers itched to get at this, to sort, assemble and otherwise bring order out of this chaos. But I knew that was impossible at the moment. It would take too long. Now I must get on with the business at hand.

Reluctantly I walked on, promising myself that some day, when I had six or seven free hours ahead of me, I would help Dearsir out by putting his tool house in order, so he could find things when he wanted them. Entering the cabin, I looked through cupboards and boxes for the chicken feed, finding it shortly. Surprisingly, and totally unlike the tool house, here in the cabin everything was in order, and shining clean. There's no accounting for men, I thought. Some men, anyway. And of these Dearsir was assuredly one. My mind touched lightly —and a bit fretfully—on the matter of my assessment work.

I went out to the fenced chicken yard, watered and fed my temporary charges. They fluttered and squawked wildly on seeing a woman approach and enter their sacred purlieus, but I paid them no mind. If there is any living thing sillier than a chicken, I have never met it. After putting the chicken-feed can away I glanced around the room looking for old newspapers. Wonderful! A whole stack, none dated less than two weeks before. I took what I could comfortably carry. On my way back to the main road I dug up a few iris rhysomes I saw near the gate. I am a natural born flower thief. I'd risk arrest any time to filch a slip or bulb that has caught my fancy—through a fence, along a walk in a public park, anywhere. I suffer a sort of moral blackout when I covet a flower.

My pockets bulging with loot and my arms full of old newspapers, Vicki and I left Bent Pine and went home. Several hours of daylight remained. I would tear up the newspapers, put the result to soak overnight, make a bucket of thick flour paste, and be ready next day to stuff the cracks against my enemies, the rats and mice that robbed me of my sleep. Then, forever free from those pests, how sweet would be my rest through the long, quiet, peaceful nights.

Nine

———◆•••▶———

NEXT morning I was out of bed earlier than usual, in spite of the fact that the rats had awakened me several times during the night. Hurrying through break-fast, I set about my task of converting newspaper pulp and flour paste into papier-mâché. A messy task, but soon done. I began stuffing the holes up around the eaves. That done, I proceeded to fill every chink I could find in the walls, then at the edges of the rough, hand-hewn boards that formed the floor of the main room. Again I became aware that this part of the cabin had been built before there was a sawmill in the whole Klamath Forest—more than a hundred years ago, I guessed that was. Would my work on it today last that long—be keeping rats out for someone in the year 2053? Startling thought, but unlikely. However, on the chance that I was building for posterity, I went back, checked every possible spot for gaps, however small, found a few and chinked them tight.

When I finished it was mid-afternoon and I had gray papier-mâché in my hair, on my face, arms, and hands, and even a generous sprinkling on my shoes. Nor did Vicki escape my spatterings. She had a sort of salt-and-pepper look. The next two hours were spent cleaning us both up to the point of respectability once more.

Sinking into bed shortly after dark, completely exhausted, I looked forward with certainty to a night undisturbed by squeaks, patterings and tail thumpings. After two hours or so of restful sleep, I was awakened by a new sound, one I had never heard before. I could not account for it. It was not loud, more like a gentle gnawing than anything else. It sounded intermittently but persistently from every direction, and seemed to be coming from just outside the cabin walls. It didn't sound dangerous, even to Vicki, who paid no attention to it, so I dropped off to sleep again.

Next morning I rose, and with the burning pride of an artisan who has done a good job, I went to look again at my defensive handiwork of the day before.

Never was I made more vividly conscious of the Biblical saying, "Pride goeth before a fall."

Many of the holes I had so carefully filled with homemade papier-mâché now gaped back at me, wide open once more to the free ingress of mountain air—and of course, rats and mice as well. I quickly arrived at the only possible explanation; my enemies had feasted royally all night on what to them was a delicious and exotic food, flour paste flavored with printers' ink.

I sat down and cried in disappointment, frustration, anger, and discouragement, doomed to endless nocturnal torment by those damnable rodents. Vicki pressed against my knees, offering her sympathy without having the faintest inkling of what caused my tears. I patted her head, found a facial tissue, blew my nose and felt better. Well, if I had to live with the rats, I had to live with them and since I could do nothing to keep them from eating up the rest of my papier-mâché there was no use crying over spilt milk. With which mixed metaphor, I rose and cooked myself a good breakfast. That day I spent working in my flowers, but when next morning came I realized that I had better get down to Bent Pine and water the boys' vegetable garden, as the weather had been warm and dry for several days. I'd bring back some eggs, too, as I had only one left. Vicki and I started in a rush of enthusiasm; I, hoping to get the job done and be back in my cool, shaded cabin before it got uncomfortably warm, Vicki because going anywhere with someone who loved her was always fun.

As things turned out, I was considerably longer in getting back than I expected.

About half way to Bent Pine I met Frenchy, book in one hand, garlic bulb in the other, coming from the direction of Happy Camp, which seemed strange at this hour of the morning. He greeted me with a jumble of words that sounded like "Bon jour, Dear Madame—bon jour, mon ami—the morning, it is joli, n'est-ce pas?"

Quite clearly, he was a little drunk, but I didn't mind. After three days during which I had not spoken to a human being, a slight case of inebriation wasn't going to stop me from enjoying a brief conversation with Frenchy. We both stopped.

"Where've you been?" I asked, thinking he would say Clear Creek, which was a mere two miles away.

"I come from Happy Camp, Dear Madame," he replied, making a futile effort to achieve complete sobriety on the instant. "I went there yesterday to see a picture show."

"Why didn't you come back last night?" I inquired. "You could easily have caught a ride."

"Couldn't get around to starting back till this morning," he said, swaying ever so little. "But—what brings you out so early?"

I found myself pouring out the story of my defeat by the rats. He nodded in the proper places, shook his head sympathetically where that motion was appropriate. I finished with a diatribe against all rodents in general and those of the Klamath Forest in particular.

"Oui, oui," he agreed. "Too bad. If only you had added

mustard to the papier-mâché, you would have had no trouble at all. I, Madame, have had experience."

"Really? But I have no mustard."

"I have perhaps half a can of it. This I will bring to you later in the day—along with sufficient newspapers for your purpose."

"You are indeed a friend," I said gratefully. "I'll be back at the cabin about four." He waved his hand in farewell and set off down the road toward his cabin.

Vicki and I proceeded on our way, and finally arrived at the gate across the short roadway that led to the boys' cabin. There I was horrified to see that the whole flock of leghorn hens had escaped from their pen and were busy doing what they could to demolish the garden patch. I flung the gate open and ran toward them, uttering bloodcurdling yells.

Evidently these hens were used to yells—much louder than mine and mixed with strong, abusive words. They didn't so much as turn their heads my way, but legged it across the neat rows of vegetables. As I came nearer, I saw that not all were running. Some stretched on comfortable beds, dusting themselves in the friable soil of the melon hills. Others were picking out tiny radishes, or nipping off the heads of the small cabbage plants.

"Sic 'em, Vicki!" I shouted. "Kill every darn chicken!"

Of course Vicki knew I wouldn't stand for that. She was the most intelligent dog I ever saw. There were, however, exciting moments while she rounded up those dastardly fowls. Chickens squawked and flew toward their pen, but no further. They ran crazily up and down the wire fence. I called Vicki off and waited hopefully for the creatures to go back through the hole they had come out of—a ragged hole made by their own efforts. But could they see it? Not one of them. They ran past it—back and forth, back and forth, getting wilder and crazier every minute.

I soon lost patience with their folly and began throwing rocks. They scattered like leaves in the wind. I tried artifice, creeping up to them with clucking noises and dulcet chick-chicking. They couldn't, or wouldn't hear me. I think chickens are deaf on and off at will. Desperate now, I picked up a pole and tried scooping them into their pen. I cornered a few and threw them over the fence, but by this time every hen was a crazy loon. I found out later that fowls belonging to men are as frightened of a woman as a woman would be of a cougar in the woods. I'd simply been scaring them into idiocy.

It was evident I wasn't getting anywhere with brute force. It behooved me to use diplomacy. I got some wheat from the bin and scattered it along a trail that led into the pen. While I rested and mopped my face—they picked up the wheat and went docilely into the pen through the wide-open gate. I closed it and started to patch the hole in the fence. At sight of me bending close to the ground, my skirts fluttering in the upriver breeze, the hens flew with outlandish squawking to the farthest corner of the pen and beat off their feathers against the wire in a frenzy.

It is a psychological fact (or would it be physiological?) that a hen has only a bit of pulp for a brain. But it doesn't help to know this when you're trying to get a hen back where she belongs.

The hole mended as best I could, I went inside the pen and to the chicken house to get the eggs I needed. This panicked the poor dumb things all over again, but I had them where I wanted them now and just let them panic. I gathered up a dozen and a half eggs and took them into the boys' cabin, putting six in a paper bag so I could take them home with me. These would last me until the boys returned.

Then, as really literary writers like to say, at long last I went out and irrigated the garden, running water down the rows, keeping it from breaking through the ditch banks by judicious use of a hoe Dearsir had left leaning against a fence. This took me some time, but I did a thorough job. This monotonous task bored Vicki after a time and she left me, but I knew she wouldn't go far. Finally I realized I had better go or I might miss Frenchy when he brought the mustard and newspapers. I shut off the water and went into the cabin to get my sack of eggs. I spied a magazine I hadn't seen, lying seductively on the table. Now I swear I hadn't been looking at it more than five minutes until I heard Vicki barking at something on the little road leading to the cabin. She wasn't upset or frightened, but spoke in a friendly, coaxing way. I grabbed the sack of eggs and went out to see what was happening.

One glance was enough. I had forgotten and left the gate open. The goats were walking daintily but purposefully toward the vegetable garden. I knew I was to blame for their intrusion and that it behooved me to act with judgment and tact.

I approached the goats like a friend. I called Vicki to my side, reached out my hands toward them with petting gestures, put a lot of sugar in my voice and backed slowly through the gate in the direction of the main road. The nannies turned and followed me, expecting something more tangible than sugary words—carrot tops and cabbage leaves, perhaps.

After the docile little creatures were out on the road I closed the gate and sat down on a bank to rest and meditate about the joys of rural life. One little kid reared herself on her hind legs, planted a small hoof on each of my shoulders and gazed into my eyes with her big, soft pale orbs, as big as quarter-dollars and a lot more appealing.

What with nannies, kids, Vicki and myself, we were pretty well distributed over the road at this point, when a fine big, glistening car swung quietly around a curve and was almost on top of us before we saw it.

Ten

———◆◆◆◆———

HE driver blew his horn sharply and the goats scattered. A lovely young woman put her head out of the window.

"Stop for a minute, Richard, dear!" she called. "Aren't these goats pretty? They remind me of Switzerland! I want to look at them."

At that moment she saw me.

"Oh, Richard!" she cried out delightedly. "Here's the goatherd, too! A woman!" She said the next few words in French. "She's just too picturesque, with her white hair and these white goats—with a background of these wonderful mountains. Oh, I must get a picture of them. A native, isn't she?"

Richard replied in French. "Maybe you'd better ask her permission before you start snapping. These natives are sometimes quite sensitive about having their pictures taken. Remember that mountain guide at Interlaken?"

The lady seemed to give up the idea of taking my picture and leaned out of the window, speaking to me most graciously.

"Your little goats are so pretty. You and the nannies make a beautiful picture with this grand view. I know you must love the nannies and I'm sure they love you too."

"Yes, they love their friends," I said, as two of the nannies pressed close to me. "They make fine pets."

"Do you drink their milk? I've been told it's very good."

"It's delicious!" I said heartily, making amends for past mistakes.

"Do you make cheese—for sale? I'm very fond of goat cheese. You know they make it in Switzerland—maybe you've heard of Swiss cheese. We've just come from abroad —and this is *so* like Switzerland—without the Jungfrau, of course."

"We have Shasta," I murmured. I could see she was working up to that snapshot she wanted—and very diplomatically, I had to admit.

"You'd make a lovely picture with your nannies." She was charming and ingratiating.

"Don't you think I should be young, with a feather in my cap, and playing pipes?" I asked demurely. *She won't dare do this to me.*

She flashed an amused look at her husband. "I think I can get the picture," she whispered in French.

"I think you'd better give it up, baby. I can see she doesn't like the idea. Besides, we've no time. We must catch that plane—and we're late now."

Sweetly, she gave up to her husband without protest. He started the car. She turned around in her seat to look back and I saw that she was watching me as they drove away.

I was well on my way homeward, leaning on a little staff I had picked up, looking, I am sure as picturesque as all get out, but feeling very old and tired. Chicken-chasing had well-nigh proved my undoing. When I came to a bend in the road I saw that the long, low car had stopped and the lovely lady was pointing a camera at me.

All fifteen of the nannies, the pretty young ones in the lead, tapering down to the old brown nanny in the rear with her ugly udder and scrawny hide, and an indeterminate number of gamboling kids, were following me in orderly procession, their heads held high, stepping as daintily as ballet dancers. Yes, if I had been a youth with pipes at my mouth and a feather in my cap, it would have been a picture worth preserving. But as things were . . .

Well, she got the snapshot, anyway.

For a few moments after they drove on, nostalgia threatened to overwhelm me. Switzerland! Interlaken! The Jungfrau!

I hurried home to my task of making mustard-flavored papier-mâché and stuffing rat holes. Frenchy, cold sober by this time, his mood not as sparkling as usual, brought me the materials that, I hoped, would finally do the trick. After supper, I again shredded newspapers, put the pieces to soak, made another bucket of flour paste, and fell into bed, too tired to care what high carnival the rats might hold.

What they really did, their appetites merely whetted by their gluttony of the night before, was to eat the rest of my papier-mâché out of the holes, leaving them clean and ready for the next treatment.

In the morning I stirred Frenchy's mustard into the paste, mixed it with the newspaper pulp. The result looked—and smelled—infinitely worse than the first batch. I filled all the holes, tamping the stuff in with a stick. The mustard worked. That night I slept in heavenly, blissful, undisturbed silence—until about three in the morning. Then I wakened, but briefly, hearing the noise of the boys' jalopy rattling by on its way to Bent Pine. Vicki heard it too, and thumped her tail on the floor in welcome. They're home, I thought, and tomorrow—tomorrow I would definitely put an end to this mystery about my assessment work. I would ask questions and insist on plain answers. What *were* they up to, anyway, treating me in this fashion?

And then I slept again, so soundly that I didn't hear the swift, pelting, but brief downpour that turned the ground to mud. Waking to bright sunshine, I was surprised to see the trees, as well as my vines and flowers, jeweled with sparkling drops of water. Breakfast over, I wandered out into the garden.

Anemones were poking pale leaves through the wet earth. Virginia stocks, in all their brilliant colors, bloomed on the lower terrace, croft lilies lifted their still tightly closed buds in the front yard, and double pink hollyhocks raised gaily dressed spikes higher than my head. The earth was too wet for me to do any work in the garden today. I'd putter around in the cabin, perhaps start to read my last Book-of-the-Month selection.

Just then the boys came up the trail, talking and laughing.

"Morning," I greeted them. "Can I get you some warmed-over coffee?"

"We've eaten," Dearsir said, looking mysterious and going directly into the kitchen. Up'nUp followed at his heels. I went inside, not feeling as brash and determined as I had in the night. I didn't exactly ask what this was all about, but I hinted broadly that they might entrust their secret to me with confidence. I poked the fire in the stove and rattled the breakfast dishes in the pan to call attention to myself. All the while I had one ear cocked to catch any chance remarks that might enlighten me. Several cryptic phrases were said, but I could see no sense to them.

"We could use billy-goat's stake rope if we could find it," said Up'nUp. A guilty shiver ran down my spine. No, I would *not* tell them were it was. Let them find it for themselves. "It's been lost since Dear Mad'm came," Up'nUp went on thoughtfully.

Dearsir went out into the back yard, presently came in again.

"I found this rope on the woodshed," he told Up'nUp.

"It's not very thick," Up'nUp objected. "You know she's heavier than she looks."

Must be they're talking about one of the nannies, I thought.

"Oh, she's not as heavy as all that," said Dearsir. "We'll have her put on that thick red sweater of hers and a heavy skirt—"

"Are you boys talking about me?" I demanded in sudden alarm.

"Sure are," said Up'nUp. "Get your warm duds on and tie something around your head—it might turn cold up there. We're going to take you for a trolley ride to the claims."

"The—the claims?" I quavered.

"That's right," Dearsir answered firmly. "That assessment work you've been nagging us about—you're going to *see* that it's done. Then maybe we'll have peace for a while along this stretch of the Klamath River."

"Me—nagging! I never—"

"Oh, yes, you did, Dear Mad'm. Now put on warm clothes . . . or do you want us to—"

I retreated into the bedroom. When Dearsir used that tone, I had learned it was better to go along with whatever course of action he was planning at the time.

Soon I emerged, looking like a carelessly made cocoon. Dearsir picked up a chair cushion and held it against my back, while Up'nUp began tying the middle part of the rope around me.

"Just what do you men think you're doing?" I demanded indignantly.

"We're taking you up to your claim, Alpine fashion," Dearsir explained in his deliberate way. "Maybe you could make it on your own steam if the trail was dry. But this morning it's slick with mud and you'd break your neck the first hundred yards. We can't wait for things to dry out, because this is the last day of June and assessment work done after today doesn't count. I'll go ahead with one end of the rope over my shoulder, and Up'nUp'll come along behind with the other end of the rope over his shoulder—"

"But what about me?"

"You'll be dangling in between. As easy as that—just like you were a lady's reticule."

I tried to treat the absurd procedure lightly, chuckling a little at the joke. But they were not joking. They were in dead earnest. And off we started, Dearsir setting a fast pace up the steep mountain.

All went well for a hundred yards or so. Then I protested that the rope was cutting me in two.

"Ship ahoy!" Up'nUp shouted. "The riggin' ain't workin'."

He dropped his end of the rope and went leaping down to my cabin. In a minute or so he was back with a pillow from my bed, white slip and all. He shoved it under the rope against my floating ribs and told me to lean on it hard and to relax.

I leaned hard perforce, but I couldn't relax.

After a few minutes with Dearsir humping along up the steep trail, slippery with mud and slick wet pine needles, the rope over his shoulder, and Up'nUp coming behind with the rope held taut, my feet dangling when I wasn't trying to catch a momentary footing, I gasped, "Boys, I'm out of breath."

"*She's* out of breath!" Up'nUp exclaimed derisively. "Why, Dear Mad'm, you haven't climbed a step!"

"I've—I've—been trying awfully hard to," I continued to gasp.

"Well, stop trying," said Dearsir. He picked up his end of the rope and started up the trail. I went with him, of course, being fastened to the rope.

I'm no lightweight, even though I am only five feet two, and I saw that Dearsir was beginning to sweat. It was coming through the back of his shirt. I was sorry to see him straining at the rope, but the only thing I could do about it was to use a little subterfuge.

"Please, Dearsir, I've lost a shoe!" I called.

"When did that happen?" demanded Up'nUp as if I had caught him in a lapse of duty.

"Back there when you skipped me over that big boulder."

"Hold up there ahead! Our passenger has lost her shoe!" he shouted. "You rest, Dear Mad'm, while I play 'hunt the slipper.'"

He went away laughing and in a minute, came bounding back. "Full speed ahead!" he shouted to Dearsir, picking up his end of the rope.

"Didn't you find the shoe?" I quavered, knowing the value of shoes in the mountains.

"Sure. I have it here in my pocket. One foot's all that you need, anyway—at a time. Don't try kicking the boulders out of the way. They belong here. You may lose your other shoe, too. Just relax, Dear Mad'm, and trust Dearsir and me to do the climbing."

Smart chap. I knew he had guessed that I lost that shoe with malice aforethought.

We continued for another half-hour over big and bigger boulders, up and down steeper and steeper gulches, across bedrock cuts. Sometimes on brief level spots I tried trotting along to keep out of the way of Up'nUp's long legs that were always pressing close behind. I wondered at their tirelessness. As we climbed higher, it grew surprisingly cooler, as they had said it would. I was glad I had worn my red sweater and tied a woolen scarf about my head.

Finally we came to a small level space. Dearsir loosened the rope from around my midriff, tossed it and the pillows down on the ground. "We'll pick them up when we come back," he said. "Here's your shoe. You are going to walk the rest of the way."

"Walk!" I squeaked. "Up this mountain? You boys know I can't——"

"Look ahead of you," admonished Dearsir.

I looked. From where we stood a wide smooth trail, evidently recently constructed, stretched ahead and wound out of sight around a shoulder of the mountain. It was a far better trail than the one twisting up from the road to my cabin.

"Go ahead," Dearsir directed. "Half a mile more and we'll be at the claims. It's easy walking all the way."

"You rapscallions!" I said severely. "Letting me worry about my assessment work, when all the time you were doing far more than the law requires, building this trail. I could spank you both!"

"The idea ain't practical, Dear Mad'm," Up'nUp said. "And please don't dawdle. We've got a day's work ahead of us at the claims."

"Just a minute. There's one question I want to ask you boys," I said, pulling my clothes straight. "How did you get the idea of bringing me up here this way?"

"Hold the *National Geographic* responsible," Dearsir answered. "We'd never have thought of it if we hadn't read in that magazine about two Alpine climbers who carried an injured man down a mountain that way. I knew we'd have no trouble carrying a little woman like you."

"No trouble!" Up'nUp exploded. "If she'd been one pound heavier she'd have had me buffaloed."

We started walking along that good, easy trail, Dearsir in the lead, with me coming next, Up'nUp following.

"We're going to wash out some gold for you," Dearsir said over his shoulder, "from your own claim. Not that it's necessary as far as the assessment work is concerned—that's all done and the notice made out, ready to send to the Bureau of Mines in San Francisco. I have it in my pocket. All you have to do is sign it tonight when we get back to your cabin. Then

I'll put it in the mailbox for Tom to pick up in the morning. But we thought you'd like to see a little gold taken from your own claim."

"Yeah," Up'nUp said from behind me. I could tell he was grinning in his small-boy fashion. "That's what we've been up to the last few days. I fixed up a sluice box and riffle, Dearsir ran a fire hose over from the main flume and put our new Little Giant nozzle on it. I sure hope we make a big haul for you."

"We can't count on its being much," Dearsir said, cautious as always. "You never know—"

"It won't bother me even if you find very little today, boys," I assured them. "Even a little will be very exciting."

"You know what Dearsir and I are going to do?" Up'nUp broke in. "We're going to extend this trail all the way to your cabin. Then you can come up here on your own power whenever you want to."

"You boys have thought of everything. I'm awfully grateful." And a little ashamed, too, I thought, remembering how cross I had been with them because they wouldn't discuss my assessment work with me. They had wanted all this to be a surprise.

We paused a minute to rest.

"And another thing," Dearsir began, looking embarrassed as he always did when I thanked him for something he had done, "if there's time, I want to take you over to the old Siskiyou Diggings. It isn't far. The gulch has been deserted for more than sixty years, but it's a great sight still. Over a period of about ten years large amounts of gold were taken out there. Those were the days . . . and who knows, they may come again, bigger and better than ever. The gold's still here. All we need is money for development. But come on."

After a while Dearsir stopped.

"Well, here we are," he said.

I looked about me. So this was my placer claim; twenty acres of gulches, boulders, bushes and great trees, tipped at an angle of approximately forty-five degrees and slanting down toward the Klamath River. Just beyond, dipping into other ravines, lay the claims belonging to Dearsir and the other three members of our little group.

Dearsir and Up'nUp worked their own claims, did the assessment work on the others. Dearsir held the power of attorney to manage all the claims, sell them if he received what he considered a good offer. That "good offer" was actually what all of us—possibly except Dearsir—dreamed about and hoped for. None of us, either individually or collectively, had available the large amount of money necessary to work the claims on a big enough scale to make them really pay. Gold was there along the Klamath in practically every shovelful of dirt, but in very small amounts. I had known all this for some time, but it hadn't really sunk in. Now, however, I was to learn it by experience. When you learn something that way, you *know* it.

Eleven

FOR the next two hours I was left pretty much to my own devices. Dearsir went to work washing down a steep bank with a stream of water shooting out of the Little Giant nozzle to chase the gravel into the sluice box. Up'nUp, armed with a heavy shovel, battled the muddy mixture, keeping it moving until it seemed to me that it all went out with a rush and fell on the tailings pile in a small gulch below.

I wanted to ask questions, but the men ignored me completely. After a while the water coming out of the Little Giant lost its force, dwindled to a trickle. The men went up to the flume to find out what was causing the trouble. As soon as they were out of sight I picked up a castoff shovel and began investigating the burlap-lined sluice box for nuggets. It was most discouraging. I didn't find any.

The boys were coming back. I turned guiltily.

"Hi, there!" shouted Dearsir. "What the heck you think you're doing? Digging out riffles and tearing up burlap isn't helping any!"

"She's running all the gold into the dump!" yelled Up'nUp.

What gold? I thought, and replied defiantly, "You've been washing gravel and dirt through this sluice box for an hour, and I haven't seen a nugget yet!"

Both men stared as if they had just discovered me and weren't particularly happy with their find.

"You don't know a nugget when you see one." Dearsir was plainly exasperated. "Look." He picked up a gold pan, leaned over the sluice box and brought up something pinched between his thumb and forefinger.

"I have here a piece of gold," he said. "I'm going to drop it into this pan from the height of one foot. If it's heavy enough to make a click when it hits, it's a nugget. Listen, now."

I listened. There was a faint click.

"Let me see it, please."

Dearsir held out the eighteen-inch iron gold-pan for my inspection. I finally managed to locate a piece of yellow metal about the size of a pinhead.

"That?" I asked.

Dearsir nodded.

"Let her pan some gold," Up'nUp suggested. "Would you like to do that, Dear Mad'm?"

"Well—yes—I guess so." I was completely deflated by that infinitesimal bit of metal that had been respectfully referred to as a nugget.

Dearsir dipped a panful of water, mud and gravel from the sluice box, swished it around a few times to show me how, then handed it over. I soon found there was a lot more to panning gold than waggling a pan. Dearsir watched my awkward movements for a few minutes, then took the pan away from me. Quickly, expertly, he sloshed the gravel and dirt over the side with a series of circular motions until only about a tablespoonful of black sand remained in the bottom. Dearsir pulled a magnifying glass from his pocket, made a careful inspection, then handed the pan to Up'nUp.

He, too, squinted earnestly at the black sand.

"Damned good," was his enthusiastic verdict. "There's five nuggets, one of 'em worth all of ten cents. And quite a showing of flake gold—probably there's some dust in it, too. Now, Dear Mad'm, what do you think of that?" he demanded triumphantly.

I looked downcast. I couldn't help it. Without waiting for

my answer he turned, threw the contents of the pan back into the sluice box.

"Great heavens!" I cried. "Why all the work of getting me up here to see you wash gravel and then throw the gold away —pffffft! Just like that!"

"Up'nUp didn't throw it away!" Dearsir defended his partner. "We'll recover it when we make the clean-up tomorrow. You've evidently got a lot to learn about placer mining, Dear Mad'm. Well, we took care of the trouble up at the flume. Let's get back to work, Up'nUp."

Once more Dearsir aimed the Little Giant at the gravel bank and the stream of water tore it down, sent mud and gravel flowing through the sluice box. Bored and completely let down by placer mining, I wandered off in search of wild flowers. The delicately exquisite wild iris were gone, but I gathered handfuls of wild syringa and lovely blue-and-white myrtle. When I came back the sun was straight overhead.

"Time to eat lunch," Dearsir announced. "You go shut off the water." Up'nUp legged it up the slope in the direction of the flume. Soon the Little Giant ceased to hiss angrily, hung limply from the empty canvas fire hose. Up'nUp came back. We all sat down in the shade of a fir tree and ate hearty, man-sized sandwiches and boxed cookies from the store at Happy Camp. I couldn't remember ever having partaken of food that tasted better. Mountain air is an unsurpassed appetizer.

The boys rested a short while, then went back to work. I lay down, my head pillowed on a scraped-up mound of pine needles and went to sleep, lulled by the busy hissing of the Little Giant, the swish of gravel and the sound of the summer breeze going its gentle way through the branches overhead.

It must have been two o'clock when I woke and sat up. The boys had knocked off work and were emptying the fire hose of water, getting ready to put it away in the crude little shelter they had built for it.

"We'll be through in a minute!" Dearsir called. "Are you ready to go see the old Siskiyou Diggings now?"

"I am indeed." I scrambled to my feet, feeling frisky as a kitten. But I quickly discovered that my kitten days were far gone. My joints were stiff from lying in one position so long. However, I got them limbered up before the boys, busy with their work, noticed my brief difficulty.

"I'll finish clearing things up," Up'nUp offered. "You two go along. I don't care if I never see the Siskiyou Diggings again. The place looks dead and finished."

"It may look that way to you, but it doesn't to me," Dearsir declared stoutly. "There's plenty of gold there still. Come on, Dear Mad'm."

The sun had dried the ground so there was little danger of my slipping. Dearsir took a firm grip on my arm and we were off. We crossed a couple of gulches, climbed a bit, and there we were, looking down on a vast, rugged, savagely colored ampitheater in which no green thing grew—the old Siskiyou Diggings. Great cliffs still showed deep wounds where streams of water had battered them, eaten into their vitals, pouring from iron nozzles so large that it took two men to direct them.

There were piles, hill-size, of red, yellow, jade, and black tailings, and great gashes in the earth where water, after having run through sluice boxes, had dashed down the slopes toward the Klamath River. It was a scene majestic in its desolation, one Milton might have used to illustrate Paradise Lost. All around, the somber green of the forest edged the rim. The declining sun touched the rocks and ledges with gold and rose, cast purple shadows under the steep cliffs. The whole vast excavation seemed to glow and burn with light. It was like an immense, fiery jewel set in dark green onyx.

"Beautiful!" I said. "And sort of frightening, too."

"A lot of work and hardships, triumphs and disappointments were lived through down there," Dearsir said. "There were no roads here then—not what we would call roads today. But over rough, narrow trails they brought in huge machinery, food, and supplies for hundreds of workers; engineers and other technical men, Kanakas, Chinese, Negroes, white men. Day and night this place boiled with activity, the night shift working by the light of enormous carbon lamps set on high poles. The electricity to run them was made right here, of course. Many a broken, burned-out stick of carbon I've picked up down there. And they took out gold—lots of it."

"Then why did they desert the place, leave it like this?"

"Well, as near as I can find out—it happened close to sixty years ago, remember—one winter there was a terrible rainstorm here on this part of the Klamath. There's never been a rainstorm like it since. The great flumes—some of them miles long—were washed out. Machinery rolled down, was covered by tons of earth and boulders. The electric plant, even the roads and trails, were swept away, obliterated."

"But greater disasters than that have happened—people have rebuilt, begun again—"

"That's right. And all that could have been done here—but the management got into a hassle as to how it should be done. Their fight became more important to them than the recovery of the mine. So the company was wrecked. But the gold is still there, Dear Mad'm—don't forget that. Someday the old Siskiyou Diggings will be worked again."

"Maybe," I said dubiously, my eyes on the desolation spread out below me; a desolation so complete that it looked as if it belonged on some dead planet. "But it won't be in my time—and I don't think in yours, either. Come, let's go back."

Silently we made our way to where Up'nUp was waiting for us. I walked down the good trail the boys had made for me. When it ended there was—greatly to my relief—no talk of taking me the rest of the way dangling on a rope. Dearsir grasped one arm, Up'nUp the other. They skipped me over the worst places, let me walk when the going was better. Soon we were at my cabin door, where Vicki welcomed us with wild barks and much leaping about.

"Will you boys come in?" I asked.

"No, thanks," Dearsir answered. "You need to rest. Tomorrow Up'nUp and I will clean out the riffles and burn the burlap in a kerosene can so as to get the gold dust that's caught in it. Tomorrow evening, if that's all right with you, we'll have the final cleanup here in your cabin."

"That'll be fine," I agreed, beginning to feel excited once more. The words "final cleanup" sounded wonderful—and important. "You boys better come for supper. This calls for a celebration."

"Yes, Ma'm!" Up'nUp said, his eyes shining. It took so little to make him happy.

"We'll be here," Dearsir promised. I signed the papers for him. "And thank you, Dear Mad'm. But don't go getting your hopes up. There may be no more than twenty-five dollars' worth."

Next day I made the cabin spotless, put everything to rights: magazines and books in place, wild flowers here and there in Mason jars and jelly glasses. I even polished the old stove. Since no meal in the Siskiyous is considered worthy of the name without beans, I put a large pot of them on to boil early in the morning. At noon I added chili powder, bacon fat, and onions, set it on the back of the stove to simmer.

I made a three-layer chocolate cake, putting it together with thick, fluffy vanilla frosting. Having no fresh meat, I decided to serve hash, using the contents of a can of corned beef, adding a judicious amount of cold boiled potatoes and finely chopped onion. This went into the oven to be baked to a crisp brown, top and bottom. Dearsir had lived in the wilds so long that he preferred canned peas to fresh ones right out of the garden, so I opened a can of them for his special benefit. These things, with coffee, would make a feast.

Evening came, and with it the boys, crowding into the little kitchen where I was putting the finishing touches on dinner. I looked at them searchingly. They weren't, as far as I could see, carrying anything.

"Where's the gold?" I asked anxiously.

"Don't worry, we have it," Up'nUp replied casually.

I turned to Dearsir. "It's in my pocket," he said. "Where's dinner?"

"Right here." I turned back to the stove with a sigh at the ways of men in general and these two in particular. I knew I'd get nothing out of them until they were ready to talk.

We ate quickly, and for the most part in silence. We washed the dishes and put them on their shelf. This last was necessary so we would have room for what was to follow.

What was to follow?

I hadn't the faintest idea. Finally when everything was shipshape and the kitchen table bare, Dearsir took a wooden box, perhaps five by eight inches square, from his coat pocket. Good gracious, I thought, my heart beating faster, could it be full of gold?

I was soon disillusioned.

Dearsir set the box on the table, opened it, and took out the most perfectly made balance-type scale I ever saw. He hung shallow brass pans on its two arms, watched them rise and fall until they came to a perfect balance, then lifted from the box a number of weights graduated in size to balance anything from an ounce to an inch-square scrap of writing paper. These he wiped with a bit of clean chamois skin, to remove every particle of dust. I watched these preparations with fascinated curiosity.

"Now," he said, and took from another pocket a family-size aspirin bottle. Through the clear glass I caught the gleam of

gold—lumps of beautiful, magic gold. For the first time I realized that the spell of gold transcends its intrinsic worth. I had at this moment no thought of what this shining metal would buy. I was conscious only of its beauty, of its ancient spell over the hearts and minds of men. I thought of the great civilizations of the past in which gold had no intrinsic value— was never sold—but men loved it, held it sacred, died for it if the need came. Strange . . .

My thoughts returned to the present and to Dearsir. He put the one-ounce weight in the little pan on the right. It bobbed down until it struck the base of the scale. Then, carefully, he poured little uneven blobs of gold from the aspirin bottle onto the other little pan until the two hung exactly level with each other. He motioned me to hand him a coffee cup, and dumped the nuggets into it. Twice more he weighed out an ounce of nuggets, leaving only a very few in the bottle. He weighed these also.

"How much?" I asked, my eyes round with excitement. At that moment I might possibly have been able to add two and two, but certainly not two and three.

"One hundred and six dollars—maybe a mite more," Dearsir announced.

"Why!" I gasped. "That's wonderful! All that from my own claim—and only one day's work—"

"You forget that Up'nUp and I worked for a week, getting ready," Dearsir reminded me. "But that's just the nuggets. We still have the amalgam."

"What on earth is that?"

"Quicksilver after it has picked up gold dust from the black sand. But there wasn't much dust this time—ran more to nuggets. Happens that way now and then. Up'nUp, show Dear Mad'm the amalgam."

Up'nUp fished around in his pocket, brought out a dirty gray ball about the size of a walnut. I took it in my hand. Soft enough to squeeze out of shape easily, it had a grainy feel as if sawdust had been worked into the quicksilver until it was like putty.

"That rough, scratchy stuff is gold dust," Up'nUp said. I felt doubtful about this unprepossessing gray lump. It didn't look as if it had the most distant relationship to the gleaming nuggets in my thick old coffee cup.

"Build up the fire in the stove, Up'nUp," Dearsir directed. "There's such a small amount of this I can use the little retort I made myself to recover the gold. We'll have a button in no time."

"Button, button, who's got the button," I muttered, not having the foggiest idea what he was talking about.

Up'nUp shoved two sticks of pine wood in the firebox of the stove. Dearsir produced a strange crude object from a paper bag he had set down by the door when he came in. It consisted of an inch-and-a-half length of ordinary water pipe with a bottom screwed on it and a wire bail on top. This hung like a tiny bucket from a two-foot-long iron rod having a wooden hand-hold at one end so it could be grasped easily.

More curious by the minute, I watched Dearsir carefully line the little bucket, bottom and sides, with cigarette papers. Squeezing the gray ball into proper shape, he put the quicksilver, or amalgam, or whatever the right name of it was, into the little receptacle dangling from the end of the iron rod. By this time the fire was crackling busily. Taking off one of the front stove lids, Dearsir lowered the little iron bucket (excuse me, retort) into the flames. Soon fumes curled out into the kitchen—choking fumes. I opened the back door and we breathed more easily. I looked at Dearsir enquiringly.

"Heat is vaporizing the quicksilver," he explained. The light of the flames cast strange, leaping shadows on the ceiling. We might have been a group of necromancers, or evil magicians, from the looks of things.

Soon there were no more fumes. Dearsir leaned over, peered into the little retort.

Twelve

———◆◆◆———

M INUTES went by. There was no sound except that made by the burning sticks of pine. Finally Dearsir spoke.

"Got a tin pan I can turn it out on, Dear Mad'm?" I got one from a cupboard, set it on the table. Dearsir lifted the soot-blackened little retort from the fire, held it for perhaps a minute, then turned it upside-down over the tin pan. A round, slightly rough piece of gold clattered out. It lay there, gleaming softly in the light of the kerosene lamp, a faint gray drift of powder surrounding it.

"The cigarette papers," Dearsir explained. "They burned, making a film of ashes that kept the melted gold from sticking to the retort." With a pair of tweezers he lifted the fast-cooling button to one pan of the scales and weighed it.

"How much do you think it's worth, Dear Mad'm?" he asked, with a quizzical grin that said plainly, Of course you haven't the least idea.

"Close to ten dollars," I answered confidently. He looked at me in surprise.

"A lucky guess," he said, a little crestfallen.

"Nothing of the kind," I retorted. "I've seen and handled many ten-dollar gold pieces before Uncle Sam called in all the gold coins and buried them at Fort Knox. Not luck, but experience, boys, experience," I said loftily.

They laughed, but there was a quality of respect in their laughter. I wasn't as dumb as they had thought.

"What are you going to do with all this gold?" Dearsir asked.

"Oh—I'm not sure, yet," I said cautiously, having no idea what people did with gold that hadn't been made into money. "Have you any suggestions?"

"You can send it to the mint in San Francisco," Dearsir said, "and get its full value in paper money. Or you can sell it to the storekeeper at Happy Camp. He won't give you quite as much as the mint will, but the difference is small. Another thing, you can trade it for what you want just as it is, at Happy Camp."

"I'm not going to sell it," I said. "It's much more exciting to trade your own gold for what you want, than sell it for plain ordinary money."

"All right. Only take good care of it until we can take you to Happy Camp," cautioned Dearsir.

"I certainly will. And thank you boys so much for everything. These last two days have been wonderfully interesting to me. And all this gold—"

"It isn't much, really." Dearsir looked at me seriously. "It seems more important than it is because you never saw gold in its raw state before. But you wait—when we sell the claims, we'll all have a great deal—not of actual gold, but of money. What you looking so glum about, Up'nUp?"

"Well—now—" he squirmed uncomfortably. "I'm not sure I want to sell. I like this country—and I like working out of doors—and there's always the chance you'll strike it rich some day. Hell, what would I do with a lot of money if I had it?"

"Oh, you're crazy," said Dearsir goodnaturedly. "Come on, let's go and let Dear Mad'm rest." He carefully packed the delicate little gold scale and weights back in its box, and they said good night.

Long after they were gone and I was lying quietly in my bed, I remembered how Up'nUp had looked when Dearsir spoke of us all having a great deal of money. Again, I heard him say, "Hell, what would I do with a lot of money if I had it?"

Maybe you've got something there, my boy, I thought sleepily, and knew nothing more until morning.

After the excitement of cleanup day several weeks went by without much happening on my stretch of the Klamath River—just day after day of heavenly weather, tending my garden, and watching the comings and goings of the many varieties of birds that inhabited this part of the Forest. Jays flashed their blue wings and assaulted my ears with their harsh squawks. A pair of brilliant yellow-and-black orioles hung their strangely elongated nest in the oak tree above my cabin and raised their family of four lively babies. Tiny wild canaries, looking like animated bits of sunshine, dashed here and there, chirping sweetly, and sometimes, aloft in the blue sky, a buzzard, made beautiful and mysterious by distance, soared and floated with no apparent effort. Slender, iridescent hummingbirds poised in mid-air to dip nectar from the white croft lilies in my garden and the wild honeysuckle that hung over the bank. Ruffled pink hollyhocks, with centers of yellow pollen that tempted the great velvety bumblebees to over-eat, unfolded their petals on thick green spikes that stood taller than my five-foot-two.

One Sunday the boys came by in their jalopy and took me down the road to see Fuchsia Point. It wasn't far—I could easily have walked, going by myself—but I think they wanted to watch me when I saw it for the first time, a hundred-foot cascade of brilliant bloom. They pretended to find my uninhibited enthusiasm over the wild beauties of the

Klamath Forest vastly amusing, but I saw through them.
They loved it all as much as I did.

But as soon as we started rattling down the road, I knew
something was wrong. Up'nUp was silent, and Dearsir looked
positively sunk in gloom.

"What's the matter with you two?" I asked.

"Nothing," both said as one man.

"Now, boys," I said, "that's not true and we both know it.
You may as well tell me, for I'll give you no peace until you
do."

"All right, Dear Mad'm," said Up'nUp. "But it's going to
make you feel bad. Three of the nannies have disappeared."

"Only two," Dearsir corrected. "We found the other one—
or what was left of her."

"You mean something has been killing them?" I gasped.

"That's right," Dearsir said, looking straight ahead. "We
missed the first one not long after you came. Then, a few
weeks later we noticed that another one was gone. We blamed
some careless hunter, or a no-good miner who wanted a mess
of goat meat. But yesterday we found one of the nannies up
near the mine. She was dead. Only her heart and liver had
been eaten. Then, the—well, whatever animal killed her,
covered the rest over with leaves and branches. She hadn't
been dead but a few hours."

I could hardly bear it. The pretty, gentle little nannie.

"What are you going to do?" I asked.

"Nothing we can do," Up'nUp answered. The—whatever
varmint done it, is smart. We'll never catch sight of it, not in
a hundred years—unless by chance."

"Look here," I said firmly, "you boys know what animal
killed that nannie. You're hiding it from me. I'm no child.
Out with it, now."

"All right," Dearsir said, swerving the car to avoid hitting
a rock that had rolled off the cliff we were passing. "We're

pretty sure it was a cougar. It's a habit of theirs, if they make a kill and aren't very hungry at the time, to eat the heart and liver of their victim, then cover the rest up and leave it. Maybe they come back to it, maybe they don't."

"Another thing makes us think it's a cougar," Up'nUp said, "is that the nannies have been killed about a month or six weeks apart. Cougars, they stake out hunting grounds, sort of, about sixty miles long, then make the rounds every six weeks or so."

"There's a fifty-dollar bounty for males—sixty for females," Dearsir said. "I sure wish we could get this one. But there's small chance of that. They're smart, those buggers."

Suddenly I remembered something. My heart gave a queer little twist.

"What kind of tracks do cougars make?" I asked.

"Oh—sort of round—not long like a dog's," Up'nUp said.

"Do—do cougars have toenails?" I quavered, then held my breath for the answer.

"Why—I guess so," Dearsir said. "They're cats, so they must have toenails. But, funny thing—their tracks never show the marks of any. I sure hope I don't lose any more of our nannies."

"Well, here's Fuchsia Point," Up'nUp broke in, as if glad to leave the unhappy subject of lost nannies. For a moment I was tempted to tell the boys about the tracks in my back yard, and then, a few weeks later, at the foot of my trail. But I was afraid they'd laugh at me, say that no cougar would ever come so close to a human habitation. And maybe what I'd seen hadn't been cougar tracks . . .

I pushed all such ideas out of my mind—and was immediately enthralled by the extraordinary beauty of Fuchsia Point. Wild fuchsia bushes were scattered about singly and in clusters all over our mountains wherever there was a seepage of water. But here at Fuchsia Point they completely covered the towering, almost perpendicular precipice with their gracefully drooping branches and massed crimson blooms, each flower pendant on its own long slender stem. The boys assured me that nowhere else on the River did wild fuchsias grow so closely massed or blossom in such profusion. They made a wonderful tapestry of color which was a delight to my soul.

The Monday following our little excursion, the peaceful, happy monotony of our days was broken. Dearsir received a letter from a man in San Francisco, saying he was interested in buying our claims—all five of them—and wanted Dearsir to come to San Francisco and talk the matter over with him. He was anxious to close the deal as soon as possible and hoped the matter could be settled in a few days.

The boys came down and told me all about it, brought the letter for me to read. Both were excited and showed it; Up'nUp by being extra talkative and exuberant, Dearsir by being more uncommunicative than usual.

"Well, what do you think of it?" Up'nUp demanded as I dropped the letter in my lap. "Isn't that great? Wants to close the deal as soon as possible. Well, so do we."

"I thought you didn't want to sell the claims, Up'nUp," I said.

"I—oh, well—I got a new angle on it. If we should sell 'em, I'd buy some more—so would Dearsir—neither of us wants to give up mining—but there'd be some extra money for— well, for . . ." He stopped, his face slowly flushing to a deep red.

"He means there'd be some extra money for Nora," Dearsir broke in.

"Yeah—then maybe she wouldn't mind staying down here on the Klamath most of the time."

"What do you think, Dearsir," I asked.

"Might be all right. Won't do any harm to go see the man."

"From the tone of his letter, seems like he has plenty of money to invest," I said. "What are you going to ask for the five claims?"

"All it looks like I can get."

"What have you in mind?" I persisted.

"Good God, Dear Mad'm, I haven't anything in mind—now! How can I have, until I talk to this fellow?"

Dearsir was right impatient with me, and justly so. I reminded myself that sometimes silence is golden. This was clearly one of those times. I poured each of us a cup of coffee and in a few minutes the tension brought on by our hopes and excitement at the possibility of selling the claims, of having oodles of money, left us and we became our everyday selves again. It is much easier to get used to the idea of being rich than it is to having that idea, once it is firmly implanted, snatched away from you.

"I've decided to go tomorrow morning," Dearsir announced. "I want you to go along, Up'nUp. The mine can take care of itself for a few days."

"Gee whiz!" Up'nUp exploded, spilling coffee as he poured himself another cup. "A trip to San Francisco! I haven't been there for more'n two years. Gee! Think I can get into my suit, Dearsir?"

"Probably. Unless you swell up and burst with excitement before we get started."

Up'nUp grinned amiably. He was too happy to mind sarcasm, especially from Dearsir who never meant it, as he well knew.

"We'll be driving into Happy Camp this afternoon," Dearsir said, turning to me. "If you need groceries to see you through until we get back—"

"I'll make out a list." I scribbled half a dozen items on a scrap of paper, handed it to him. He rose.

"Come on, Up'nUp, we better get going. Thanks for the

coffee, Dear Mad'm." They went out and I watched them hurrying down the trail.

Money, I thought. How would it seem to have money you really didn't need to buy the comforts and a few modest luxuries of life? You already had those but money to spend for slightly mad indulgences like a trip to Hawaii, or—or a mink coat . . . but I had never wanted a mink coat—didn't now. Oh well, I'd have no trouble thinking of ways to spend it, once I had those thousands of dollars.

The boys brought my groceries that evening and next morning before I was out of bed I heard their jalopy go rattling down the road.

The next few days restlessness possessed me. A woman of my expectations couldn't be expected to weed a pansy bed, rake the walk leading to the shower, pick up dead leaves. What *could* a woman in my position do? Not much of anything, it seemed, except read the magazines Tom left in my mailbox—and wait for the return of the boys.

Then, on the fourth night of their absence, just as I was dropping off to sleep, I heard the familiar rattle of the old jalopy as it went by.

"Well, they're home," I said to Vicki. She corroborated the statement with several joyous thumps of her tail. She knew the sound of the boys' car as well as I did.

Next morning when the boys came up my trail on their way to the mine, I was out in my garden pinching off faded blossoms to keep my plants a-blooming.

"Good morning!" called Up'nUp, not too cheerfully I thought. "Hope you're okay," and he would have let it go at that if I hadn't stopped him.

"Come over here, boys," I called, "and tell me about your trip. What happened in San Francisco? Did you sell the claims?"

"No, we didn't," said Up'nUp shortly.

"That's too bad. Stop a minute and tell me about it. Being part owner, I have a right to know—isn't that so, Dearsir?"

Dearsir's face took on the withdrawn look that he uses when he has no intention of talking, but I saw that Up'nUp had something to say.

"We-e-ell," he began uncertainly, "it was this way. Things didn't seem to go the way Dearsir thought they ought to and—"

"Oh, I see," I interrupted with a short laugh. "Dearsir, did you go and ask the buyer some outrageous price?"

"Nothing of the sort," Dearsir said sharply. "Just why do you take for granted that I wrecked the deal?"

"Well, I thought—maybe—you asked an unreasonable price." I knew by the way Dearsir's eyes flashed that I was getting on dangerous ground.

"I do not overestimate the value of the claims!" he protested. "I quoted a very conservative price—$50,000, one-third down, the rest on a long-term note."

"Fair enough," I said judiciously, knowing nothing whatever about it. "Well, you had the power of attorney from all the claim holders—why didn't you go ahead and close the deal?"

"Because, dear Mad'm, when it came to a showdown, the man had only five hundred dollars in cash—wanted to pay the balance on a percentage basis—I mean, a percentage of the gold he took out."

"My goodness! Only five hundred dollars! After all the big talk in that man's letters! I hope you told him what you thought of him, causing you to drive all the way to San Francisco."

"I told him," said Dearsir grimly.

"He sure did," Up'nUp grinned. "You should have heard him. He said—"

"No need to tell Dear Mad'm everything you know," said

Dearsir sourly. "We better get up to the mine and do a little work on the flume for a change." They started up the trail.

"How are you getting along at your claim?" I called as an afterthought.

"Fine!" Dearsir yelled back. "Putting in that new flume and getting everything ready to start washing gravel by the first of December is a big job, but we'll make it."

As soon as they were gone, the thought of Those Tracks bobbed into my mind, and I felt scared again. Still, I couldn't make up my mind to tell the boys about them. Finally I decided that when they came down the trail this afternoon, I'd make them a proposition, but wouldn't tell them what was back of it. Of course, maybe they wouldn't agree.

The midday heat of summer beat down on the Klamath River country, which is cut off to some extent by high mountains from the Pacific breezes. Between ten and three Vicki and I retreated into the cabin. Shaded as it is by two great trees, it is always cool there. By early afternoon my front yard lay in the shadow of the mountain and a cool breeze came wandering up the canyon.

I put on my flamingo-pink smock and Paris-green garden hat. This shocking mixture of colors, bought in haste, had one advantage; it always spurred me to action if I wasn't feeling up to the mark. The heat had made me listless, but after I dressed up in my store gardening clothes, I felt better.

The flowers were thirsty, so I started by wetting down all the beds thoroughly. Vicki followed me about to watch, and occasionally to gulp water from the stream flowing out of the hose. This took quite a while. Then it occurred to me that I had better make a close examination for bugs, worms, and a kind of tiny white fly that sometimes hid under leaves, feeding voraciously. I got down on my knees, then flattened out to be nearer the warm, fecund earth that so generously nourished my flowers. Slowly I inched along from one plant to the

next, turning leaves over, picking the crowding soil away
from the stems with a hairpin, petting them with loving
touches. The drowsy afternoon slipped by. I became wholly
absorbed—deaf to the sound of the mighty river flowing past,
the song of birds, the occasional swish of a passing motor car.
Only a green thumber of the first order knows the exultation
I felt that warm summer afternoon; the thrills of the ardent
flower lover, the ecstasy that is heaven-born. The shadow of
the mountain crept across the river, began to climb the opposite canyon wall.

Into that tiny paradise there suddenly broke a metallic,
whirring noise, deadly, insistent—something to rasp the
nerves, send chills to the stoutest heart. I knew I must spring
away from this noise—but I was prostrate, paralyzed with
fright, my stiff joints and unresponsive muscles refusing to
lift my weight from the ground. I was lost.

But I had forgotten Vicki. She had been lying near me. At
the first sound of that deadly buzz, she jumped to her feet,
stood stiff-legged in front of my flowers. She began a thin,
broken, high-pitched barking, a call for help. Above her ap-
peal rose the terrifying sound like the exhaust from some unearthly machine.

Suddenly Vicki sprang back with a wild bark of joy. Dearsir came running down the trail. He had heard Vicki and
knew by the tone of her bark that she had "treed" a rattler. He
came springing into my garden.

"Your gun—where is it?" he demanded.

"Table—kitchen—" I gasped.

A moment later he had it in his hand, stood facing the
flower bed the awful sounds were coming from.

"Sic 'em, Vicki," he said.

She lunged at the bed with a furious bark, sprang back as
the snake lifted its ugly head to strike. Dearsir fired a shot that
split the snake's head open.

I staggered to my feet, sick and faint—no doubt looking like something a car had run over on the road. Muddy, hat askew, face smudged, hands black with dirt, my gay pink smock crusted with mud.

Dearsir said, with a fine sarcasm he always has handy when he needs it, "Most gardeners can get close enough to their work without lying on their bellies. As a temptation to rattlers, you've got the world beat." He pulled the still-writhing snake out of the flower bed by the tail, walked close to the edge of the garden, and threw it with all his might into the river. That done, he stood there for a moment, looking down.

"Well, I'll be damned," he said at last. "Billy's stake rope—hanging on a wild lilac bush. I thought I'd left it on a fence post somewhere." He turned and gave me a suspicious stare. I had a sickly grin on my face. He'd caught me and I knew it.

"Women!" he said.

I thought I'd try a little palaver.

"You made a wonderful shot. Thank you for killing the rattler and saving my life."

"You're welcome," he said gruffly, but I wasn't fooled. His gray eyes were twinkling. Now what was it I had planned to take up with him? Oh, yes. And now was the time to do it, with the snake episode playing into my hands.

"Do you think, Dearsir," I began hesitatingly, "what with rattlers and—and things—that it might be a good idea for me to have that big gun that's leaning against the wall at Bent Pine? You never use it."

Stony silence for a moment. Then Dearsir unlimbered.

"Great God, Dear Mad'm! You'd be killing somebody with that thing! Up'nUp or me, as likely as anybody else—no, come to think of it, you wouldn't either. You could barely lift it off the floor, much less point it at anything. If having it here will keep you from being scared of the dark, I'll bring it over."

"Thank you," I said, with pretended meekness. "I *could* rest it on the window sill to shoot it, you know."

"Don't try it. You're to have it just as an ornament."

"Yes, sir."

"I'll be going down the road to Frenchy's tonight late and will leave it at your front door. You can get it in the morn-ing."

I will get it tonight, I thought.

He turned to leave. But halfway down the trail to the road he turned.

"Better take a snort of your snakebite medicine, Dear Mad'm," he called. "It'll do you good, even though the snake didn't bite you. But after this, when you're out of doors during rattlesnake season, keep on your feet. Snakes are where you find them, and sometimes they find you first."

Though his voice was faintly admonishing, it was also kind. Now I knew that he did not wholly despise me for being ig-norant and careless about rattlers. I think he may have even forgiven me for disposing of billy goat's rope.

But I couldn't forget the snake, nor the possibility that at any time I might hear the terrifying sound of another rattler ready to strike at me with his deadly fangs. I hated to feel that I must continually be on the alert for the danger underfoot when I longed to gaze at the trees, the birds, the blue sky. But I knew I must be watchful from now on until cold weather, when the snakes would slither into their holes for the winter.

And of course, I was still faced by that matter of *the tracks.*

Thirteen

———◆◆◆◆►———

AS SOON as it was dark I went to bed, blew out the kerosene lamp and waited for the big gun to be left at my door. I wanted Dearsir to think I was asleep, so he wouldn't come in with a lot of instructions and advice as to what I should do with it. I had my own notions about that.

Shortly after nine o'clock I heard footsteps, then the sound of something heavy being set down quietly beside my front door. The steps receded. I waited fully ten minutes. Then, taking my flashlight, I opened the door. There stood the gun —and beside it a box of cartridges. I looked—yes, the rifle was loaded. I felt a warm glow of satisfaction. This was Dearsir's way of saying he trusted me with this fearsome weapon, and I was to use it as I saw fit.

I lugged the gun inside—it *was* heavy—and went back to bed, but not to sleep. Thoughts of the lost chance to sell the claims haunted me. I ticked off one by one the many pleasant things I could do and have, if and when those claims were sold. But of course when the five claims were lumped together in a package, the price was so high that it made most people think twice.

Then, a scintillatingly brilliant idea occurred to me. Why

not sell the claims one at a time, to different persons? Surely, more people could be found who had money enough to buy one claim than to buy all five. The plan looked foolproof to me, and I thought pityingly of the ineptness of Dearsir and Up'nUp in not thinking of this idea themselves. "Men," I told myself smugly, "certainly don't have as much ingenuity as women. I'll tell the boys about it when they come by in the morning. They'll like the idea, I know."

Once more I began to plan what I would do with the money from the sale of my claim. This proved to be so deliriously fascinating that hours went by before I dropped off to sleep. Consequently, when I woke the sun was far up in the sky and the boys had long ago gone up the trail to the claims. No matter, I thought. This evening when they come by on their way home will do as well.

After breakfast I picked a dozen or two ripe apricots and noticed that the enormous peaches on the tiny trees were beginning to color where the sun touched them. The rest of the morning slipped quickly by, as I watered the flowers on the two terraces below my front yard.

Around two o'clock Millicent arrived for one of her infrequent visits, bringing me a tight bunch of slightly limp purple pansies. I found two empty jelly glasses in the cellar, loosened the stems and put the flowers in water, where they soon perked up, holding their little faces proudly erect. I noticed with surprise that she was wearing lipstick. She was growing up—no doubt about it.

Millicent and I never lacked for subjects of conversation, despite the difference in our ages, for when I ran down she prodded me with questions about the world outside which she had never seen; about San Francisco and cities still farther away, where I had been many years before.

This afternoon we finished inspecting the flourishing chrysanthemum plants bordering the path to the shower, and sat down on the wash bench. The singing of the River furnished background music for our talk.

"Have you ever been to London, Mrs. Patterson?" she asked.

"Once. But it was very long ago—I was about your age."

"Oh, do tell me about it! Was it foggy? Did you see the changing of the guard?"

"It was drizzling rain—and I don't remember that I saw anything very interesting—except the Queen, of course."

"Oh! Queen Mary! What did she—"

"Not Queen Mary. Queen Victoria."

Plainly, it took the child a moment to adjust herself to a time so long ago. "You really saw her?" she asked in an awed voice.

"Well—briefly. I was going to school in London at the time. Along with my classmates, I was taken to see the sights, among them the Queen as she passed by in her carriage. We stood for a long time in the rain and bitter cold. Next to us were a dozen or so small Eton boys, all dressed up in starched Eton collars. Of course they must have had on jackets, too, but I only remember those cold linen collars when they needed furs. I forgot to bow when the Queen passed, I was so busy looking at a black crocheted fascinator she wore on her head, instead of the crown I had expected. The instructress who stood beside me knocked my head down with 'Bow to the Queen, you stiff-necked American!' Which I immediately did, with great respect."

"I wish I could see a queen," Millicent sighed.

Well, I thought, that's quite a wish for a little girl living in the Klamath Forest, but maybe it will come true—who knows?

After she had gone I went into the front yard and sat down on an old stump there, keeping watch for the boys. I could hardly wait to tell them my wonderful idea about selling the

claims singly, instead of a group. I even planned to be mag-
nanimous—say I was willing they should sell their claims
first—I'd wait for a buyer to come along for mine. Below me
the Klamath whispered and murmured on its swift way to the

distant sea. The breeze made a sighing sound through the branches of my tall fir tree. Flowers bloomed at my feet and peace seemed everywhere.

Then I heard footsteps on the trail above me. Soon Dearsir came in sight—alone.

"Where's Up'nUp?" I asked in surprise.

"Gone-to-Yreka," he said, as if it were all one word, and went striding past without a pause.

"You come right back here and tell me what happened!" I cried. "He didn't say anything when he was here yesterday about going to Yreka—or anywhere else."

Dearsir turned. "Tom left a letter for him in the mail box this morning," he said morosely. "From Nora. He threw some clothes into a grip, got into the jalopy, and took off. Said he'd be back in a few days."

"But why? What was in the letter?"

"Darned if I know. Sometimes that boy talks too much and again he talks too little."

"You could have asked him."

"I don't ask anybody about their private affairs, Dear Mad'm."

"Very creditable, I'm sure." But the sarcasm was lost on him. He was evidently put out by Up'nUp's reticence, so there was no use pursuing the subject further. I was dying to know what had taken Up'nUp to Yreka and Nora so suddenly, but I'd just have to wait to find out. Suddenly I remembered my wonderful idea.

"Dearsir, I've been thinking it will be much smarter for us to sell the claims one at a time. You see . . ." I launched into an enthusiastic description of my plan and how I was sure it would work out. He let me go on babbling for fully a minute before he stopped me. Of course I'd about run down by then, anyway.

"Dear Mad'm," he said patiently, "how much do you know

about conditions under which placer mining is carried out here along the River?"

"Why—why—nothing," I stammered, "but I'm not talking about how to work the claims—only about a way of selling them."

"Same thing. You have to move a lot of gravel and dirt here to get even a little gold. It costs money to build flumes and sluice boxes, buy hose and giant nozzles. You have to have a big area to work or your investment won't pay off. So we sell the claims together, or we don't sell them."

"Oh!" I said, thoroughly deflated, my dreams of a spending spree from the sale of my claim disintegrating into the ether.

"Now don't you worry," he said, seeing my disappointment and awareness of how foolish I had been. "We'll sell the claims yet—get a good price for them, too. There's plenty of gold there, but it takes more money than we have to get it out economically and in really paying quantities. In the meantime, Up'nUp and I aren't starving to death, and you aren't depending on your claim. You're not even having it worked. Just be patient, Dear Mad'm."

He was right—I wasn't depending on the gold from my claim to keep me from starving to death—but I was counting on it to make some rather extravagant dreams come true—and he talked of patience—something I knew nothing about except from hearsay.

The next night Up'nUp came back from his visit with Nora. But he wouldn't talk about it, not even to Dearsir. Just said he'd gone to Yreka to get some things straightened out. I found his silence on the subject very hard to bear. One morning when he brought the goat's milk I rushed in where any self-respecting angel would have feared to tread.

"How's Nora?" I asked.

He almost dropped the empty glass jar into which he was supposed to pour the milk.

"Oh—why—well, she's all right." He put the empty jar on the table, picked up the full one and started to walk away with it.

"Come back here with my milk, Up'nUp," I said sternly. "Doesn't Nora have week ends off from her job in the telephone office? I wish she'd come to see me sometime."

Consternation showed in his face.

"Oh, no, Dear Mad'm! I don't want her doing that. I told her on no account—"

"I suppose she won't, then," I said grumpily. I really wanted to see Up'nUp's wife and get to the bottom of his most peculiar behavior toward her.

Every week or ten days after that, Up'nUp would disappear for two or three days—gone to see Nora, Dearsir would report, refusing to discuss the subject further. Up'nUp became alarmingly serious. No longer was he boyishly gay and noisy, whooping like a wild Comanche as he half fell, half ran down the steep trail from the mine. Once I asked him why he didn't buy himself some new jeans to replace the ragged ones he wore. He said. "Oh, these will do me for a long time yet. I'm saving—"

"What's more important than a pair of jeans with a solid seat in them?" I inquired brightly.

"Well, now—I can't exactly say," he muttered vaguely and went away from me.

When I saw Dearsir I took the matter up with him.

"What in tarnation is the matter with the lad?" I asked.

"I have no more idea than you have." Dearsir looked anxious. "Must have something to do with Nora. Maybe she's after him to quit mining, get a job in Yreka and stay with her."

"More than likely. And you couldn't really blame her." I said, thinking how much I'd miss Up'nUp if he went away.

The next afternoon it looked so much like rain that I didn't start to do anything in the garden, but sat in my bedroom reading a magazine. Once in a while the low mutter of distant thunder rolled among the mountains, too far away to disturb Vicki asleep at my feet. But suddenly she came alive, gave the soft growl that meant a woman was coming up the trail. I went to the door.

A tall girl carrying a heavy suitcase came slowly up the steep path. She had black hair, milk-white skin and remarkable beauty. When she reached my doorstep she set the suitcase down. I smiled, giving her time to recover her breath so she could speak.

"I'm Nora, Mrs. Patterson," she said finally. I hid my surprise as well as I could.

"I'm glad to see you, Nora. Won't you come in?"

"Well, thank you. I intended to camp at Bent Pine with Up'nUp—I've got to calling him that, too," she said with a quick smile. "But it looked like rain and the door was locked—so I thought I'd better come down here and stay with you. Up'nUp says you're agreeable to most anything."

The thought of a house guest in my tiny cabin appalled me, but I managed a few conventional words of welcome. She accepted them at face value.

"My car's at the foot of the trail," she said. "I'd better go right down and get the rest of my stuff before the rain starts." She hurried away. Soon she was back, staggering under the weight of a sleeping bag and a large pasteboard carton in which I could see cans and jars and packages of food. Her face was flushed, her breathing heavy, as well it might be after her climbing that steep trail twice, both times carrying a heavy load.

She sank into my decrepit rocking chair, completely spent. I took a good look at her. She was probably two or three years older than Up'nUp, I guessed, but most attractive, with big Irish blue eyes in a face stamped with amiability. She seemed absolutely sure of her welcome with me—but wasn't certain of Up'nUp.

"He doesn't know about my coming," Nora said, rocking back and forth, breathing deeply. "Fact is, he told me not to. He may be angry with me for a few minutes, but he's a good guy, really. He'll get over it."

I stared at her, wondering at the almost labored breathing, interspersed with sighs of deep exhaustion.

"The trip's been too much for you," I said. "You'd better rest a while."

"I don't need a rest as much as I need a change. I get tired, staying up there at Yreka by myself, working in the telephone office, looking after chickens and garden truck in our yard there. I just couldn't be bothered with them any longer. I had a two-week vacation coming to me, so I got a boy to look after the chickens and garden—and here I am." She caught her side and winced. There was a startled look on her face that alarmed me.

"What's the matter, Nora?" I asked uneasily.

"I'm pregnant. I felt him kick just then. When he does that it makes me feel faint for a few seconds."

I sank into a chair, feeling faint myself. So that was why Up'nUp had acted so strangely. Then doubt struck me. "Are you sure? You don't look it."

"When you feel 'em kick like this one does, you're sure, Mrs. Patterson. In fact, I've been sure for several weeks. That's why Up'nUp's been coming to see me so often lately. Manlike, he's scared—for me and him both—and I guess not too happy about it . . . Do I hear the men coming?"

"You do," I said, mentally bracing myself. Nora's face brightened with a smile that was both happy and timid. She stood in the open door and called out, "See who's here! Surprised?"

I realized for the first time how tall she really was as she reached out her big, soft white hands and caught Up'nUp by the shoulders, her eyes almost level with his. He took her hands away and went into the kitchen. The rest of us followed him. What with the big old stove, the table, one chair and four people, there wasn't much room to move around. Nora and Dearsir greeted each other as if they had met before.

"Seems to me we're crowding Dear Mad'm out of her house," Up'nUp said unsmilingly. "Nora, you better come down to Bent Pine and stay there until it's time for you to start back to Yreka."

"Oh, I'm not crowding you one bit, am I, Mrs. Patterson?" she appealed to me. Then, without waiting for an answer, "I'll sleep on the floor in my bag. And I've brought this boxful of eats. Look!" She dragged out the box.

Up'nUp poked around in it. "Hm-m-m-m. Mustard pickles—sardines—crabmeat—chili sauce—pickled pigs feet. . . . Where's the substantials?" he demanded.

"Oh," Nora said lightly. "I knew you'd have all that kind of thing here. I brought stuff you especially like. Look in that brown paper parcel."

Up'nUp jerked it open. I felt ashamed of him. Nora was trying to please him, but he refused to be pleased. Six or eight thick T-bone steaks tumbled out. We gasped—all except Nora. She beamed. Up'nUp shoved the steaks aside, looked reproachfully at his smiling wife.

"You know you oughtn't to spend money—even though you do earn it yourself—on things like this—not now. There's going to be—you're going to need. . . ." He broke off, his hands shaking.

Suddenly I understood him better, saw why he was acting this way. He was frightened at the prospect of the baby, confused and made uncertain by this new responsibility that would soon be his. Somehow, he hadn't grown up yet.

I glanced at Dearsir. He looked completely baffled.

"Nora and Up'nUp are going to have a baby," I announced flatly.

For a moment Dearsir looked as if a boulder had hit him on the head. Then his gray eyes began to twinkle.

"Well, it's nice someone finally got around to telling me,"

he said. "I'm going down to Bent Pine. You come along when you get ready, Up'nUp." He strode off, whistling. Evidently he was no longer worried over Up'nUp's strange behavior of the last few weeks.

But I still had my worries, for I was in the middle of what promised to be a most unpleasant situation. What was the matter with these two nice young people, anyway? Why had they married, if Up'nUp didn't care for Nora a great deal more than he appeared to? I said goodbye to Dearsir, and turned back to them.

At that moment Nora jerked the heavy box of groceries around, started to shove it under the table. Suddenly she cried out, put one hand to her side. "Gosh!" she moaned. "Good gosh!"

Up'nUp caught her in his arms and carried her to the bed. He did it right tenderly, too, and rested a gentle hand on her shoulder until she stopped gasping for breath.

"You stay there, now," he said gruffly. "I'll help Dear Mad'm cook some of those steaks—we've got to eat 'em before they spoil—and I'll get Dearsir back up here to help us. You keep quiet, like I tell you."

She smiled at him, love in her eyes. "Okay, you big lug," she said, giving him a smart slap on the knee that would have knocked me to the floor. "Step lively. I'm hungry."

A short while later we all sat crowded around my kitchen table, eating a delectable dinner of fresh corn and peas picked half an hour before in the garden at Bent Pine, steaks cooked exactly right by Up'nUp, hot biscuit by me, and for dessert, canned pears sprinkled with chopped mint leaves from the patch growing around the water barrel in my back yard. Most of the dishes were chipped, few of them matched, but more delicious food could not have been found in any restaurant in the land.

The men washed the dishes, Nora dried them. When the task was finished, Up'nUp's thanks to the beautiful Nora was a resounding slap on the buttocks. This was the nearest thing to a caress I ever saw him give her, but who shall say that his love for her was not tender and true? It took me a little while to understand this, but I finally did.

The men gone, I pushed Nora's sleeping bag into a corner

and we shared the bed. Much to my astonishment, I didn't mind. I liked Nora from the first moment I saw her, and though some of her ways astonished me, I came to love her very much.

There was no more talk of her going down to Bent Pine—there was no room for her there, anyway—and we spent a pleasant two weeks together. The boys ate dinner with us every night and it was all fun—at least for me. I watched the tension ease out of Up'nUp's face, heard him laugh again. I think it helped him when he saw me take the situation as a matter of course. He seemed to get used to the idea of having a son—neither he nor Nora ever considered anything but a boy—and toward the end of Nora's visit he began to act as if he felt a little proud.

"What are your plans, Nora?" I asked her one day shortly before her vacation came to an end. "You can't keep on working much longer. Are you going to the hospital in Yreka to have your baby?"

But Nora was unconcerned. "Oh, I don't know," she said. "There's lots of time. Why worry about it now? Everything will be all right. Thank you, Mrs. Patterson, for letting me stay with you. You've sure been sweet to me." For a moment her eyes were wistful. "I feel a lot better about—well, about everything. And Up'nUp does, too. Don't you worry."

Well, I didn't—exactly. But I couldn't help thinking about her—and the baby—and hoping everything would turn out all right. I loved them both so much, Nora and Up'nUp. Then a strange and moving thought swept over me. Nora's and Up'nUp's baby—why, when it came it would almost be as if I were a grandmother.

Fourteen

———◆◆◆———

AFTER Nora went back to Yreka we settled down to routine living again. The warm, languorous summer was upon us, but we loved it. Frenchy strode by now and then on his various comings and goings, clad only in a pair of old jeans haggled off above the knees, probably with a dull knife, and heavy shoes. The boys piled up gravel at the mine in preparation for the time when they could wash it through their sluice boxes. They built more flume so that more water would be available. And they worked on the trail at odd times, determined to make a way up to the mine that I could cover on my own power. This last seemed rather impractical to me, but I hoped they would succeed. It has always been hard for me to stay away from places where important things are going on. And washing out gold was certainly important.

Several times one or the other of the boys brought me wild blackcap raspberries—a lunchbox full. What I couldn't eat, I canned in pint Mason jars, storing them in the cellar.

I felt peaceful and happy—except that in a small corner of my mind there still lurked the threat of Those Tracks. I kept a sharp lookout for them wherever I went, but saw none. However, the fact of their absence did not lull my anxiety regarding them nearly as much as the sight of Dearsir's big rifle standing in the corner of my bedroom.

The peaches, grown to enormous size, turned brilliant red where the sun touched them, shading to a cool green where they were covered by the close-curled leaves. Magically, they grew soft, filled to bursting with sweet juice. One day when I was in the woodshed, I heard a soft plop! as one fell to the ground, unable to cling to the tree any longer. A moment later brakes screeched on the road below, followed by the sound of a car door opening. Then came the chatter of astonished voices. I tiptoed to the edge of the yard and peered down between the interlaced branches of fir and oak and maple trees.

A man stood on the roadway, holding my big, luscious peach in his hand, staring at it. The peach had evidently dropped at the very edge of the yard, then rolled down the pine needle-covered slope and onto the road.

"Where on earth did that come from?" he was demanding of the universe. A woman leaned out of the car window to look. "In the middle of the Klamath Forest—the biggest, most beautiful peach I ever saw, rolling in the middle of the road! *Rolling*, mind you!" He sounded angry, the way men do when something happens they don't understand.

"Why, that *is* odd," the woman answered in a high, carrying voice.

The man walked about, looked up and down the road, glanced in my general direction. I could see him plainly, but I knew he'd have to have sharp eyes to see my cabin through the thick branches; or me, as long as I didn't move. I hated to lose that peach, but it was worth it to see those two mystified people. Finally the man climbed back in the car, peach in hand, still shaking his head. Then the car was off with a clashing of gears and a splutter from the exhaust.

I went over to the little tree and tested the grip of every peach to the parent stem. One came loose in my hand, but the rest held tight. After that, every morning I tested each beautiful crimson fruit until the last one was ready to be eaten. I didn't propose to puzzle any more motorists—or lose any more peaches. One was enough.

But before my peach crop—if thirteen peaches can be called a crop—was harvested, a responsibility beyond my wildest imaginings was laid upon me.

I was called on to perform a major operation.

I call it a major operation, because it is customary among people I know to speak only of major operations. Heaven only knows what a minor operation is. I have never heard anybody say they had one. But a major operation, if my understanding of it is correct, is one that causes a lot of inconvenience, fear, and pain. At least, I have heard it expressed that way by people who have had major operations. I notice that these people always have happy memories about their operations, though, and like to mention them whenever the opportunity offers.

Personally, up to the time I was confronted by the necessity of performing one, I was not acquainted with operations, never having had a major—or even a minor—one. *Umberuffen.* (This word, if spoken quickly, keeps evil spirits away. I also knock on wood as an extra precaution.)

Like most disasters, this one struck suddenly. It was between the time I ordinarily awakened and the time when the boys usually went by on their way to work—that is, it was broad daylight and I was fast asleep. The first indications I had of untoward events was Dearsir banging on my door and Up'nUp calling hoarsely, "Dear Mad'm! Help! Let us in!"

I piled out in a hurry, slipped into my old blue robe, and opened the door. Up'nUp's face was a dull red, his eyes round and frightened. Dearsir had the washed-out appearance of an overripe summer squash. Both men looked as if they'd had an all-night session in a Happy Camp pool hall.

They barged inside and stood panting from their run up the

hill. I'd never known Up'nUp to drink anything more power-ful than beer, but I had misgivings when I saw his bloodshot, bleary eyes and unsteady walk. And him about to become a father! I was really cross with him.

"Up'nUp," I began severely. "You've been drinking too much hard liquor!"

Beyond giving me a reproachful look, he didn't bother to reply, but dropped into my old rocker with complete disre-gard of its weaknesses.

"He isn't drunk, Dear Mad'm," Dearsir said. "He's a sick man—hasn't slept all night. We didn't know what was the matter with him until toward morning when I got out my flashlight and looked him over good. When I found out what the trouble was, I couldn't do a thing for him myself. We needed you. Look at him, Dear Mad'm. Isn't he a pitiable sight?"

Up'nUp groaned, flopped over on his side in my creaking old chair. He really looked dreadfully ill.

"Good heavens!" I exclaimed. "Let's do something for him quick!"

"My God, you can't be too quick for me," Up'nUp moaned, closing his eyes. "The pain is terrible. I'm as sick as a sick dog. Get busy, Dear Mad'm, and do something."

"But what shall I do?" I asked in bewilderment. "What's the matter with him, Dearsir. What's causing all this pain?"

"I think you'll have to do some cutting. As for the cause, Up'nUp, get your shirt off and lie down on your belly on Dear Mad'm's bed." Up'nUp obeyed with alacrity. "Then she can see—"

"But you must know, Dearsir," I interrupted, feeling as if I turned white, though maybe I didn't, "I'm no surgeon—not even a trained nurse. Now, Up'nUp, you get your shirt right back on. Dearsir, you take him to the county nurse at Happy Camp."

Up'nUp made no move to get off the bed, but groaned louder than before.

"You can do what's necessary, Dear Mad'm," he said. "I know you can. You've got the instruments and you've had experience with 'em. That's why I came to you—throwed myself on your mercy—"

That was all I could take of Up'nUp's histrionics.

"Keep quiet!" I turned to Dearsir. "What is the matter with him? And what is he talking about?"

"Tell her to get the instruments," came in Up'nUp's agonized voice. "And for God's sake, hurry! This is killing me!"

"What instruments?" I cried. "A butcher knife? A monkey wrench? Or maybe a hammer to knock him out with? That's all I have."

"He has in mind the tweezers in your manicure set and a fine needle," Dearsir explained. "I brought along a razor blade in case—"

"Dearsir, if this is a joke—which I wouldn't put beyond you two—I'm not going along with it. If it's serious, I'd like you to show at least as much sense as you were born with."

"Yes, Dear Mad'm." Dearsir looked down at the floor, but not before I had caught a twinkle in his eyes. "The fact is, from Up'nUp's point of view, it is serious. He got a tick in his back yesterday up at the mine, and by the time we knew what had happened the little devil had bored his head into Up'nUp's back. If you can't twist the tick's head out while holding its body between your thumb and forefinger, you'll have to pull it out with tweezers, or dig it out with a needle, or cut it out with a razor. It really isn't any fun having a tick's head buried in your back, Dear Mad'm."

"I suppose not. I'll look at his back." I leaned over Up'nUp, shirtless, prone on my unmade bed.

"You mean that little speck—looks like a mole or something? Why, it isn't any bigger than a flea—"

"Flea!" shouted Up'nUp, propping himself on his elbows and giving us furious sideways glances. "It's a damned poisonous red wood tick! And he's working his stinking head into my back deeper and deeper every minute. I'll die of blood poisoning—"

"You'll do no such thing," I said, pushing him flat on the bed again and making a closer inspection. Sure enough, there was the body of a wood tick, bright red with tiny black legs, it's head imbedded in Up'nUp's tanned back. Around it spread a dark purplish spot the size of a quarter. When I saw that, I really felt sorry for him.

I got the tweezers from the box that held my manicure set, and a bottle of lysol from the kitchen. Up'nUp was watching every move I made.

"For God's sake, don't use those tweezers, except as a last resort!" he yelled. "You'll break its head off and there it'll be in my back. You got to twist him out."

I looked inquiringly at Dearsir. He nodded. "Better try twisting him out first. I couldn't get hold of him with my big fingers, but you can do it. If you twist long enough the head will come out."

I got hold of the pesky insect with my thumb and forefinger and began to twist. Pretty soon I was all twisted up. My elbow stuck out at an angle. My fingers were in the way. My eyes were getting crossed. I let go and took a breathing spell. Up'nUp groaned again.

"Please, Dear Mad'm, try once more," he begged. "Hold onto him tighter. Twist harder. You've got to get his head out of my back. It's hell now, but it'll be double hell tomorrow, if his head stays in there. My whole back will be paralyzed. I won't be able to lift my arms. I'll be swollen worse'n a poisoned pup. I'll likely be dead. But don't bury me with this tick in me."

Suddenly I ran out of patience with him.

"Give me those tweezers," I said to Dearsir.

"Don't use 'em!" shouted Up'nUp.

"Here—go ahead," Dearsir said, handing them to me. "Pay no attention to him. He's delirious—or something."

Dearsir pushed Up'nUp down on his belly and held him there. I used the tweezers to grasp the body of the tick and gave a jerk.

The body came loose, but the head stayed in.

"Oh, I'm sorry," I said. That was a mistake.

"So you didn't get his head," Up'nUp said weakly.

"No."

"Then you got to try digging him out."

"Digging?" I asked faintly.

"With a needle," Dearsir explained. "Get a small sharp one from your sewing kit, please."

I did as I was told, then rummaged around and found my magnifying glass. With that in one hand, needle in the other, I went to work. I had no notion of having to cut that tick's head out with a razor, so I worked hard. When the blood oozed up, I wiped it off with a facial tissue and dug deeper. Now that Up'nUp was suffering real pain, he endured the punishment in silence. He didn't even flinch as I alternately probed and squeezed.

At last the tick's head came out. I swabbed the wound with lysol. Up'nUp sprang from the bed, pulled on his shirt.

"Thank you, Dear Mad'm, for performing a successful operation. You saved my life."

"Oh, come now, it wasn't that serious."

"Dear Mad'm," he said solemnly, "nobody who's never had a wood tick in his flesh knows the fix I was in. One little measly wood tick can put the fires of hell under you."

"That's right," said Dearsir.

"I'm hungry," Up'nUp announced. "Come on, Dearsir, let's go back to Bent Pine. I'll cook up some ham and eggs, you make a batch of sourdough pancakes." He dashed out the door and down the trail, followed by Dearsir.

The major operation was over. Everyone was happy—except me. I took two aspirins and went back to bed.

Fifteen

———◆◆◆▶———

B Y THE following day Up'nUp had completely recovered
from his major operation, but it took me a little longer
than that. The next week he went to Yreka to see Nora.
When he came back he told me shyly that Nora had quit her
job and had ordered the small garments and other things that
she and the baby would need, picking them out from Mont-
gomery Ward's catalogue. I got out my copy of that indispen-
sable volume and did a little ordering myself—three ridicu-
lously small lamb's-wool shirts I simply couldn't resist and a
two-compartment rubber-lined shopping-bag affair for Nora,
to hold wet and dry didies.

When the package arrived via Tom and the mail box at the
foot of the trail, I puzzled over two broad rubberized straps
inside the bag, one at each side. Then suddenly it dawned on
me that they were to hold two feeding bottles upright. I
thought of Nora's beautifully rounded body—and I didn't believe those straps would be needed. I was quite sure she
would be capable of nursing her baby. The next time Up'nUp
went to see Nora, he took my gifts with him.

For two or three weeks it rained nearly every day—not all
day, but enough to keep the air delightfully cool and turn the
trails to soft mud. One midafternoon of intermittent sunshine

and showers, I sat snug and warm in the old rocking chair, pulled close to the stove, reading a magazine, Vicki asleep at my feet. Suddenly she raised her head, cocked one ear. I

could hear nothing unusual, but she was often aware of sounds that were completely beyond my ears. A moment later she scrambled to her feet, made a rush for the front door, then looked back at me, whining. Giving her only half my attention, I rose and let her out. She shot through the door and made a rush up the trail leading to the diggings. Startled, I watched her.

Then I saw something that scared me half out of my wits— a cougar partly hidden by low brush less than a hundred feet

away. I knew instantly from the boys' description what the
great tawny beast was. Vicki began to bark wildly, but slowed
her advance, moving toward the fearsome animal one step at

a time. The creature, three times her size, came out of the
brush, turned to look at Vicki, its long tail swaying ominously
from side to side.

"Vicki!" I shouted. "Vicki! Come here this instant!"

She didn't so much as hesitate in her slow forward move-
ment toward the big cat. The cougar bared its great teeth in a
snarl, and crouched. The big gun! Now was the moment
when I must use it. Whirling, I sprang inside, grabbed the
rifle, dragged it to the door. Using the last ounce of strength I

could command, I raised it to my shoulder, aimed it as best I could at the cougar's head.

But I was too late.

At that instant Vicki and the cougar sprang at each other. There was a wild scuffle, Vicki silent now that the battle had been joined, the cougar snarling viciously. If I shot now, I was as likely to kill Vicki as the cougar. But the beast would finish Vicki quickly, that I knew. Should I fire or not? The choice was a terrible one. I hesitated, my finger on the trigger, the barrel swinging as I kept it pointed at the struggling animals, in spite of the dragging weight of the Enfield. The cougar closed its jaws on Vicki's back and began to shake her. The beast's teeth must have slipped, for suddenly Vicki sailed through the air and landed some twenty feet away. I couldn't have aimed the rifle accurately to save my life, but at that moment the cougar's head came into line with the gunsight. I pulled the trigger.

The animal leaped and fell on its side. I've killed it! I've killed it! I exulted. But the cougar got slowly to its feet, swayed a moment, then wobbled weakly into the brush. Frantically I called my little dog—and this time she obeyed me. Suddenly the gun was so heavy I could hardly lift it onto the doorstep, drag it into the cabin, lean it against the wall. Vicki came inside with me. I slammed the door shut. She was bleeding from half a dozen places. I washed her wounds with soap and water. She licked my hands while I did it, though it must have hurt her terribly.

As soon as I had done all I could for her, I began to think about the cougar. Had I killed it? I thought it very likely that I had. Surely the bullet had hit the brute's head. Vicki—brave little Vicki—she had done her best to protect me. She lay at my feet trembling, whether from the shock of her battle with the cougar, or the pain of her wounds I did not know. I shook a little myself, remembering the animal's snarling face. The hands of the clock pointed to five. The boys would be along soon. I wanted very much to tell them what had happened, start them out before dark to hunt for the cougar.

Soon I heard them coming. Stepping to the door, I called to them. They came in. Vicki did not run to them, but lay quietly.

"Boys," I said, "I killed a cougar."

They looked at me, disbelief in their eyes.

"Well, now," Dearsir began mildly, "that's a right exciting statement. Where is it, Dear Mad'm?"

"I don't know—exactly. Up on the mountain somewhere. I don't think it could have gotten very far after I shot it."

"Now, Dear Mad'm," Up'nUp said mildly. "You're fooling. You couldn't kill a cougar with that little Iver Johnson of yours. It just ain't reasonable. Maybe you shot at a bobcat."

"Are you sure you shot at any kind of varmint?" Dearsir asked. "Maybe you just thought you heard an animal in the brush—"

"I didn't 'think' anything of the kind!" I declared indignantly. "And as for a bobcat—could a bobcat have done that to Vicki?"

They went over and looked closely at her.

"No-o-o, I guess not," Dearsir said. "But you still couldn't have killed a cougar—not with that little gun of yours."

"I used the Enfield."

"Now, Dear Mad'm, don't tell us you even lifted that gun, much less aimed——"

"Look at it!" I pointed dramatically at the big rifle.

Dearsir picked it up, broke it, put the gun back against the wall.

"It's been fired, sure enough."

"Now I guess you boys will believe me. What about you going to look for that cougar before dark?"

"All right," Up'nUp said. "We'll take the gun along, just in case."

They started up the trail. It wasn't more than ten minutes until they were back, lugging the great limp brute between them. They threw the carcass on my doorstep and came in.

"It's dead," Up'nUp stated, quite unnecessarily. "And it's a female. You made yourself sixty dollars, Dear Mad'm."

That startled me. I'd forgotten the bounty. The main thing about it all so far was that I had saved my Vicki's life.

"Hm-m-m," I said, looking down at the dead cougar. "But to collect I'll have to send the hide as proof—"

"That's right. But you have no use for the hide."

"Yes, I have. It will make a nice rug to cover the floor by my bed."

"Darned if it wouldn't!" Up'nUp exclaimed. "And I'm the fella that can fix it for you, first class. You know that bearhide on the wall at Bent Pine? Well, I tanned that."

"Did a good job of it, too," Dearsir broke in. "Why don't you give that to Dear Mad'm—it's bigger—and you take the cougar hide?"

"My gosh!" Up'nUp was disgusted. "That heavy, woolly bear hide on Dear Mad'm's floor? In nothing flat it would be full of dirt and Vicki's fleas. This cougar hide will make a fine rug. Let me fix it for you, Dear Mad'm."

"I will. And thanks, Up'nUp. I really need a rug now that winter is coming on. The floor is not only rough, it's cold, too. How long will it take you to get it ready?"

"Oh, a few weeks—more or less," he replied vaguely. "I'll get the jalopy so we can haul the varmint up to Bent Pine. I'll skin it tonight."

He went loping down the trail to the road.

"You know," Dearsir said, "I'll be surprised if we lose any more nannies. Very likely this is the brute that has been kill-ing them. It's still hard to believe that you could aim and fire that big gun. Where you got the strength I don't know. Of course it took courage, too, but I always knew you had that."

His words of praise made my heart glow.

Several days later I went down to Bent Pine. There, stretched carefully and nailed securely to the outside of the cabin on the side sheltered from the rains was my cougar skin. It was all of five feet long, a nice generous bedside rug size. I was impatient to have it on my floor, warm and soft to my bare feet on cold mornings. But I couldn't get a promise out of Up'nUp as to when it would be ready.

"Takes time, Dear Mad'm, takes time," was all he would say.

Days grew shorter, nights and mornings really chilly. When I got up the morning of the first day of October I smelled frost even before I opened the kitchen window. And there it was, setting everything a-sparkle. I could see that the dogwood leaves had turned scarlet almost overnight. Would this be the end of the vegetable garden at Bent Pine? I hoped not, for when the frost killed the plants we would have to depend on canned vegetables, except when the boys went to Happy Camp and brought home what we could use before they spoiled.

This was a good morning to build a rousing fire in the big old cookstove, hover around the kitchen, and do some chores I had been putting off until there should be weather like this. After breakfast I straightened up the cabin. Chore number one was doing my fingernails which, as every well-regulated woman knows, should never be put off. But not being well-regulated was a condition on which I prided myself, a condition I had come to the Klamath Forest to attain, and my fingernails certainly showed it.

I reached for the box containing my manicure set and lipstick, which I kept on top of the cupboard. Setting the lipstick to one side, I arranged tweezers, orange sticks, file, nail polish remover and nail polish at hand on the kitchen table. Then I grasped the file and began to work on thumb nail number one.

Suddenly the boys barged into my kitchen, set their lunch pails noisily on my table.

"Top of the morning to you!" bellowed Up'nUp. "How's the world treating you this frosty morning?"

"Fine. But tell me, how is it treating your vegetable garden?"

"Not bad," Dearsir answered. "It's in a protected place, you know. The tomatoes are probably done for, but I don't think anything else was damaged seriously. We can tell better when we get home tonight."

"Will you look at Dear Mad'm?" Up'nUp marveled. "Getting herself all prettied up. You expecting company from San Francisco?"

"No, I don't expect to see anybody—except you boys," I said, industriously filing away.

"What you doing it for, then?" Men, I thought. The question irritated me.

"For fun. Just to pass the time. Because I'm a silly old woman—"

"You don't need to get mad," Up'nUp interrupted with spirit. "I was just trying to find out why women—"

"Never do it," Dearsir broke in. "There's no use, and it saves wear and tear not to. Dear Mad'm, we just dropped by to tell you that one of the nannies had a kid last night. Already, it's jumping around lively as a cricket. We'll carry it up to see you next Sunday. It can't walk this far until it's a little older."

"I'd love to see it."

The boys picked up their lunch boxes and went on their way, leaving me in my warm, cosy kitchen and to the job of making my hands look as much like a lady's as possible. Soon every nail was beautifully rounded and a gleaming rosy red. Leaving the items of my manicure set to be put away later—a besetting sin of mine, leaving things at loose ends—I went outside into the crisp sunshine and proceeded to ruin all my work by straightening up the early chrysanthemums, now blooming in profusion. By this time all traces of frost were gone. That task finished, I nipped buds off the late-blooming varieties so they would give me larger blossoms about a month later. Vicki padded after me as I moved along the rows.

Lunchtime came. I went inside, drank a glass of milk, munched a cracker, and hurried back to my task. One thing led to another. As every flower enthusiast knows, all the work in a garden is never done. It must have been about two o'clock when I was startled to see Millicent Benning's curly top, under a trim navy blue hat, bobbing along the second terrace below me. I had never seen her wear a hat before, and this one even had a tiny white veil.

In an instant I took in the rest of her clothes; a navy blue suit, transparent white blouse, pearl earrings, and high-heeled, open-toed pumps. She was breathing fast, as if she had climbed the trail swiftly.

"Oh, Mrs. Patterson!" she called. "I've such good news to tell you! I'm on my way to Eureka and I can only stay about an hour. A friend is coming here to your place for me."

"Let's go in the house and sit down so you can catch your breath," I said, genuinely glad to see her.

We went inside, Vicki coming with us, and sat down in the bedroom.

"Remind me, Millicent," I said. "Before you go, I want you to see how well the chrysanthemums you gave me are bloom-ing. They're in the back yard."

But she wasn't thinking about chrysanthemums. She wasn't —at the moment, anyway—even thinking of Emily Post.

"Mrs. Patterson," she said, still breathless, "I'm going to be married."

"Millicent! You don't mean it!" It couldn't be. This child . . .

"It's the truth. I've come to say goodbye to you and to Vicki. She's a sweet dog—aren't you, Vicki?"

Vicki responded with ecstatic hand-lickings and much soulful rolling of the eyes.

"But, dear child, isn't this awfully sudden?" I was still feeling the impact of her announcement, and for some reason tears filled my eyes.

"It's not sudden at all, Mrs. Patterson," she bubbled on. "Danny and I have known each other for a whole month. He came up here to hunt deer when the season opened. He lives in San Francisco and he's twenty-one years old, and he's six feet tall and has a good job in his father's hardware store. He wanted me to marry him when we'd only known each other a week, but we had to get my parents' consent because I'm only sixteen, and they wouldn't give it to us until a few days ago. But they like Danny and think he's all right."

"But—but you're so *young*."

"Well, I suppose so. But I know a lot more about marriage than most girls my age."

I sat there stupefied. This child—a mere baby to me—she was wildly happy—I was so afraid for her. But she had more to tell me.

"I know you think I should wait," she went on, "but you don't understand how things are. I love Danny so much—and I just have to get away—far away—where I'll never hear my father and mother quarreling, saying terrible things to each other. I want to live like nice white people do. And I'm really white—almost, anyway. Danny says people in San Francisco aren't like folks here on the Klamath—they won't care whether I'm part Indian or not. And they won't need to know, anyway."

"Has Danny told his parents?" I felt a little faint and more than a little heartsick.

"Oh, no, he hasn't told them. He wants them to see me first. I'm going to San Francisco tonight. A friend will meet me there and I'll stay at her home. Tomorrow Danny will take me to see his parents—he says he knows they'll love me. Then just as soon as we can get a license—we have to wait three days, you know—we'll be married. Oh, I'm so happy! I don't think anyone could possibly be happier than I am!"

"I'm going to make you a cup of chocolate," I said. "You visit with Vicki while I get wood for a fire."

I went out to the woodshed, found there was no kindling, and split a handful. When I came back into the kitchen I saw that Millicent had been busy—like the child she actually was. Vicki sat on a chair, her front paws resting on the table. Millicent had seen the fingernail polish where I had left it, and had painted Vicki's toenails a brilliant red. My lipstick had also been put to use. Vicki's mouth was liberally smeared and her jowls flamed with color.

"Isn't she pretty!" Millicent exclaimed. All thoughts of her coming marriage had gone from her mind and she was completely engrossed in her little-girl play.

"If Vickie was my doggie, I'd tie red ribbons around her neck," she chattered on.

Vicki drew her lips back in a doggish grin, showing her white teeth in pleasure at being the center of attention. I was more troubled than ever. As I started the fire and put milk on to heat, I thought I should at least try to dissuade Millicent, before it was too late, from the course she was embarking on.

"It seems to me, Millicent," I said, "that since you know so many unpleasant things about marriage, you'd be afraid—"

"Oh, no!" she broke in, wide-eyed and smiling. "You see, some marriages are made by the devil and some are made in heaven. Mine and Danny's will be made in heaven, because we really love each other."

I had no answer to that—at least, none that made sense even to me.

A few minutes later as I poured the steaming chocolate into cups, my hand shook a little and my heart ached for her. I would make one more try, I thought resolutely.

"How can you be so sure you and Danny will be happy together?" I asked. Serenely she answered me.

"Because Emily Post says 'Faith, hope and love will make any marriage a success.' Danny and I have all those. And she also says, 'The greatest of these is love,' or something like that, and I know she's right. Danny thinks just as I do about it."

I knew I had no argument that would stand up against this. I was beaten. I was going to lose my little friend to this stranger—this boy—who just happened to come hunting in the Klamath Forest and found this sweet young girl whose home was a troubled and unhappy one.

There came a honking at the foot of my trail. Millicent jumped up, kissed me goodbye and ran down to join her friend in the waiting car. Vicki pawed my skirt, trying to get my attention. She was most unhappy about her scarlet toenails—and so was I. If the boys came down from the mine and saw her like this, they'd never stop ribbing me. They'd believe —or pretend to believe—that I did it in a moment of complete idiocy.

I scrubbed Vicki's face with soap and water, used polish remover to get the scarlet enamel off her toe nails. But for days afterward Vicki's jowls wore a faint but unmistakable blush. I never looked at her that I did not think sadly of little Millicent and wonder if she had found love big and strong and hopeful enough to give her the happiness she longed for.

Sixteen

———◆◆◆►———

EVERY season of the year in the Siskiyous has its own
special beauty, but fall is the most striking, with its bold
splashes of color on the mountains and the deep, glow-
ing shades of late-blooming flowers in the tiny gardens
around the widely scattered cabins. The crimson of dogwoods, the yellow of maples, were everywhere, flaunting
themselves against the unchanging green of firs and pines. In
my garden yellow, dark red, orange, and bronze chrysanthemums held their heads aloft with a valiant air, as if they
knew that soon their beauty would be stricken overnight by
a sudden onslaught of winter.

But night after night went by without killing frosts, and I
treasured each day of beauty that the mild weather gave me.
There was little I could do in the garden now, except enjoy
its last riotous burst of colorful blooming. So, with idle hands,
the human mind being what it is, I began to worry about
Nora and about Millicent. Within a few days I heard from
both.

One afternoon, sitting on the old stump in the front yard,
I was astonished to see Nora, heavy and awkward now, climbing my trail.

"Nora!" I cried in consternation, "what are you doing here?

Don't you know that the baby is due almost any day now?"

She came into the front yard, panting for breath and sat down on the doorstep as if she could go no farther.

"Sure, I know it," she grinned. "Who better? But I got fed up on being alone so much way off there in Yreka, so I drove down to visit with you and Up'nUp for a few days." Suddenly she put one hand to her side, closed her eyes, her face twisting with pain.

"Good heavens, what's the matter?" I cried, having visions of the baby being born right there in my cabin.

"Oh, nothing—nothing," she said hastily, opening her eyes. "He's just carrying on as usual. Do all babies kick as hard as he does?"

"I haven't the least idea. But Nora, you shouldn't have come. What if—"

"Now don't you worry." She got up, patted my shoulder as if I were an unreasonable child. "Everything will be all right. I told you I couldn't stand being alone any longer. I'll go back in plenty of time. The doctor says I've got two weeks yet. Where's Up'nUp?"

"He and Dearsir are up at the mine. Nora, be sensible. Drive right back to Yreka!"

"Why, Dear Mad'm, aren't you glad to see me?"

"Of course I am! I've been worrying about you . . ."

"All right. I'll go down to the car and get the box of groceries I brought—"

"You'll do no such thing!" I cried. "The boys can carry it up later. Think of your baby!"

"Gosh, he doesn't let me think of much else," she said, hand pressed against her side again.

I gave up. "You better come in and lie down," I said. Maybe Up'nUp could talk some sense into her head—I couldn't. If she had her baby here it would be up to me to do whatever was necessary—and I hadn't the faintest idea what that was.

My friends and I had always availed ourselves of hospitalization; no fuss, no bother, no danger of a mishap through carelessness. Feeling most inadequate, I made Nora a cup of tea and kept her quiet until the boys came down from the mine.

Up'nUp looked at her, his face turning a dark red. "I've got a notion to spank you," he said, advancing toward her. I sprang in front of him, pushed him into a chair, for he looked quite capable of following through on the idea. Dearsir, with his usual restraint under stress, said nothing.

"You go get Nora's box of groceries out of the car and bring it to the kitchen," I told Up'nUp crisply. "We'll all have supper here. After that, we'll try to plan. She can't go back tonight —it's too late now."

Nora helped me prepare the chops and string beans she had brought and we ate in strained, unhappy silence, finishing with an apple pie from a Yreka bakery. After the dishes were washed and put away, the boys and I did our best to persuade Nora to say she would go back home in the morning. But we got nowhere. Firmly, but pleasantly, she repeated that she would stay a few days—if that was all right with Dear Mad'm. No, she didn't know how many . . . everything would be all right . . . we needn't worry. Finally the boys said goodnight. Nora and I went to bed. She fell asleep almost immediately, but I lay awake for hours, imagining all sorts of trouble and dire events.

A couple of days went by—anxious days for the boys and me, apparently happy and serene for Nora, except when the baby decided to take a little strenuous exercise. This usually turned her white and faint. But she quickly recovered, became as carefree, even gay, as ever. Darn the girl, I thought in exasperated worry. I couldn't help loving her—no one could—but I did wish she'd act with more sense about this.

It got so that my entire thoughts were given to Nora, what she was doing, what she was eating, where she was going. If she stooped to pick up a pin, I sprang forward as nimbly as my stiff joints would permit to grab the pin for her. Then a little later I might see her through the window picking up a fifty-pound sack of potatoes and lugging it to the cellar in the back yard. If she sat down suddenly, hand pressed against her side, I ran for my pint bottle of brandy and poured out a little for her. It always seemed to do her good, so I relied on it in time of trouble.

One day she took a notion to go to the mine, but said nothing about it and waited until the men were well out of sight up the trail. I saw her sneak up the hillside and shouted to her to come back, but she pretended not to hear me. The boys had mentioned to me once or twice about their working on the trail, extending it down toward my cabin, as they had promised me they would the day they had taken me to my claim. But still, I knew Nora had a long way to go over steep, rough ground before reaching less difficult going. There was no use following her. Even in her condition, huge and ungainly, she could out-climb me up that steep trail. I went back into the cabin and spent a miserable day, expecting momentarily to hear the boys coming down the trail supporting an agonized Nora about to have her baby. If ever a woman tempted Providence, Nora did. But towards evening she and the boys arrived, laughing and talking. She'd had a wonderful day, Nora said, holding boards while Up'nUp nailed them together.

A day or so later as Nora and I were washing the breakfast dishes, there came a knock at the front door. There stood a young, brown-haired Hoopa Indian boy of twenty or so, wearing blue jeans and a plaid wool shirt. A rifle swung nonchalantly in the crook of one arm.

"Good morning. You Mrs. Patterson?" he asked.

"Yes," I replied. He smiled.

"I was pretty sure this was the place," he said. "Milly Benning's my cousin. Before she went away she told me, come hunting season, I was to bring you a piece of venison."

"Why, thank you."

"Around daylight this morning I killed a nice little spike buck," he went on. "Here." He picked up a brown paper parcel from the doorstep and handed it to me. "Milly says you're her friend."

I took the package. It must have weighed twenty pounds, but I managed to hang on to it. What in the world would I do with all this meat? No refrigerator . . .

"Thank Millie for me," I said. "And do tell me—how is she?"

"Why, all right, Mrs. Patterson. I was down to San Francisco last week and went to see her. She has a nice home. I like her husband fine. They just bought a car. I guess you know Milly wasn't very happy here, but looks like now she has everything she wanted."

"I'm so glad. And thank you for bringing me such a generous portion of venison."

We said goodbye and he went striding down the trail. Staggering under the weight of the package in my arms, I made my way to the kitchen, dropped the meat on the table. Nora tore the paper off. There were steaks, chops, and a large roast, all expertly cut, ready for cooking. She nodded approvingly.

"Best-looking deer meat I've seen in a long time," she commented. "But an awful lot for four people. Let's make some of it into jerky."

Jerky? I'd read all my life of Indians making jerky back in the early days of the old West, but how they went about it I had no idea.

"By all means, let's," I agreed, with no enthusiasm whatever. "I hope you know how, for I certainly don't."

"I'm an old hand, Dear Mad'm. Didn't you know I grew up on the Trinity River not over a hundred miles from here?

Helped my pa make jerky every year until he got too old to live out in the wilds and we moved to Yreka. Of course, it has to be done right. First, we gotta have sharp knives."

Nora showed me how to put razor-sharp edges on my two butcher knives by drawing them expertly along the edge of the big old stove. Then we cut several pounds of the venison into thin strips of varying lengths, sprinkled them with salt and generous dashes of black pepper. The pepper was to keep the flies away, as well as add to the flavor, Nora explained. In a little while these strips dangled from the clothesline in the clean mountain air.

"What next?" I asked.

"Nothing—for three or four days."

When the strips were brown and bone-dry, we brought them in and packed them into some empty salt sacks I had saved. So this was jerky. I looked at it in undisguised aversion.

"But it's good," Nora said. "Here, eat a piece." She broke off a brown nubbin and held it out to me. Knowing she would give me no peace until I did, I put it in my mouth and began to chew.

"Why!" I exclaimed, "it's wonderful! I thought it would taste like raw meat—but it doesn't. It tastes like—like—"

"Like nothing else on earth," Nora said matter-of-factly. "If jerky was put in a nice package and sold at a fancy price, everybody would be crazy about it. But people think of jerky as something the poor, ignorant Indians ate when they couldn't get anything better. Hah!"

"You're so right. Give me another chunk."

It was the next day after we tasted the jerky, early in the afternoon, that Nora came into the bedroom where I was reading and sank into the old wicker rocking chair. I looked up. She was breathing fast, her hands gripped tightly in her lap. My heart lurched. The boys were up at the mine—she and I were alone—what would I do if . . .

"Nora," I said quietly, "what is it? What's the matter?"

"Oh, nothing," she said. "At least, nothing I can't handle. Guess that doctor was wrong and I've stayed too long. The baby's made up his mind."

Her hands unclenched, she breathed normally again. I sat frozen in my chair. Nora rose, got her hat and coat from the closet, put them on.

"What—what are you going to do, Nora?" I asked, managing to keep all but a slight quaver out of my voice. "You can't drive all the way to Yreka!"

"I'll go to the little hospital at Happy Camp."

"But you shouldn't even—you can't—"

"Sure I can. You've no idea how tough I am."

"But the baby's things—what you're going to need—"

"They're all in a suitcase down in the car. You don't think I'd be crazy enough to leave them in Yreka, do you? Well, I better get going."

I walked with her down to the car, sick with worry, looked up and down the road with the frantic hope that Frenchy might come along—I could send him up to the mine for the boys. But no Frenchy. Nor anyone else.

Suddenly she clutched my arm, gasped for breath as another pain washed over and through her. When it receded, she climbed into the car and was gone.

I waited in the garden until the boys came down the trail, told them what had happened. Up'nUp gulped, turned white. Dearsir regarded him grimly.

"How long has she been gone?" Dearsir asked me.

"About three hours. Of course it's only eleven miles to Happy Camp, but it's a slow road. She shouldn't have had to drive the car."

Up'nUp started down the trail on a run.

"I'll go right away!" he yelled back. In a moment he was out of sight. I sank down on the stump, my knees trembling. What had been my reasons for coming up here on the

Klamath River to live, I asked myself. So I could have quiet, peace, freedom from problems—and above all, solitude. And look what I got! Then, ashamed, I pulled myself together. I must think of Nora—she was the one who had problems. Trouble was, I could do nothing about them. If only all would be well with her—and the baby—and lovable, exasperating Up'nUp . . .

"Now don't you worry, Dear Mad'm," said Dearsir, always remarkably adept at reading my mind. "Nora's young and strong. She'll be all right. And the baby will do wonders for her and Up'nUp. They'll stop being so flighty."

But I wasn't listening. "If only she got to Happy Camp in time!" I worried. "Of course any ordinary woman would have had hours and hours—but Nora never does anything like other people. So how can we expect her to have a baby the way other women do?"

Dearsir took me firmly by the arm. "You come inside," he said. "I'll get supper for you tonight. I tell you, Nora will be all right."

Time crept by until the middle of the next afternoon. Up'nUp came bounding into my cabin, shouting, "Hi, Dear Mad'm! I've got a son! Nine pounds and seven ounces!"

"*You've* got a son!" I said, relief and exasperation sharpening my voice. "I suppose Nora had nothing to do with it. Sit right down and tell me how she is."

"Why, Dear Mad'm," his eyes were bewildered, "of course the baby's her son, too. She's fine—got to the Happy Camp Hospital in plenty of time. We decided to name him Benjamin. That's a big name for such a little tyke, so Nora said we'd call him Benji. The nurse says he's a beautiful baby."

The poor innocent. Didn't he know that every nurse worth her salt said that about every new baby? And what's more, every father and mother believed it, no matter how lacking in all but the most rudimentary human characteristics the infant might be. A lovely delusion to which every parent is entitled.

Two weeks later Up'nUp took Nora and Benji back to their little home in Yreka. It was months before I saw Nora and the baby. Up'nUp went to see them occasionally, but I could never get a really satisfactory report out of him, and Nora wasn't at her best when writing letters. I often wondered what kind of mother she made. Caring for a baby doesn't allow much leeway for impulsive action and is made up largely of drudgery, boredom and a treadmill routine. But mother-love generally carries a woman through. Did Nora love little Benji enough? I wasn't sure, but I hoped so.

Along about then there was a run of steelhead in the River, each fish making its way upstream to spawn in the creek where it had been born three or four years before. Why all species of salmon have this mad passion to return to their birthplace and there complete their life cycle and die, no one knows. Nature is supposed to be all-wise, but sometimes I wonder.

Dearsir built a tiny smokehouse at Bent Pine, with shelves of chicken wire to hold the split fish, and an iron pot at the bottom in which to build a smouldering fire of oak, madrone or alder chips. Here he smoked the fish he and Up'nUp caught at the mouth of Independence Creek, a few miles down the Klamath. The boys gave me all I could use, and the fish were delicious. Much finer and more delicate in flavor than could be bought in even the gaudiest supermarket.

With pounds of smoked steelhead, salt sacks full of jerky and many jars of wild black-cap raspberries in my cellar, I felt very much the pioneer woman, living off the country. This was true in only a limited sense, of course. Most of my food was bought in the store at Happy Camp.

Seventeen

THE steelhead run continued and city men, with expensive fishing equipment and wearing astonishing sports clothes, came to try their luck in the Klamath River. Once in a while, when we wanted fresh fish, the boys would catch a five- to ten-pound steelhead or king salmon in the big eddy a few hundred feet below their cabin. It wasn't considered a good place to fish, not like the mouth of one of the many creeks flowing into the River; but if the fish were running, the boys felt abused if they had to wait more than fifteen minutes for a bite.

The days continued to be filled with sunshine. There were a few showers in the night, but the usual hard rains held off. It was a lovely, peaceful time which I spent reading, writing letters, collecting brilliantly colored leaves from the slope above my cabin, and taking walks with Vicki down the road past Fuchsia point, or up toward Happy Camp a mile or so, where I could gather armfuls of sword ferns growing by a little waterfall.

After one of these jaunts, in which I had gone farther than usual, tempted by the old lure of "what's around the next curve," I reached home in the late afternoon, close to exhaustion. After resting a bit in my old rocker, Vicki and I ate supper as twilight slowly darkened into dusk. It was then I heard Dearsir and Up'nUp coming noisily up from the road. Must be something important to bring them here this time of day.

I met them at the door.

"Glad you're not in bed!" Up'nUp sang out excitedly. "We got something to talk to you about. Wow! Ain't we, Dearsir?"

I mentally made allowances for Up'nUp's natural exuberance. They crowded past me into the narrow kitchen and pulled chairs up to the table. Dearsir reached for a match and lighted my lamp. I prepared to listen to the usual grapevine gossip about people and happenings up and down the River.

"The claims are sold!" Up'nUp burst out. "For seventy-five thousand dollars!"

"Wh—what did you say?" I gasped. "That can't be—it's impossible—"

"It's true, though. Absolutely and entirely and gospel true."

"He's being a little hasty," Dearsir put in. "What he means is, we *might* sell them, and we *might* get seventy-five thousand for them. There's a difference between 'might sell' and 'sold.' You see that, don't you, Dear Mad'm?"

"Yes—yes, I see." But I didn't. I was groggy from the shock of Up'nUp's announcement. "But—what about the seventy-five thousand?"

Up'nUp, as always, was ready with an explanation.

"This is not exactly new to us, Dear Mad'm. Over a year ago a big San Francisco mine promoter—name of Morse—was up here and talked to us. He said he was sure he could make a deal, if the price was right. He wanted to know if we would take seventy-five thousand, lock, stock and barrel, including the cabin. We said yes, right off the bat, no dickering, no nothing. We could easy have got him up to a hundred thousand—"

"What difference did it make?" Dearsir asked. "We never

heard from him again until today. But you're telling her, Up'nUp."

"Well," Up'nUp began again, eager to finish his story, "time went by and we forgot all about it. As you know, we been pretty busy up there at the diggings. Then this afternoon, a little while after we got back to Bent Pine, Ed Sears—he lives down close to Somesbar—stopped by on his way from Happy Camp and left us a telegram that come for us there this morning. It was from Mr. Morse, and it wasn't no measly ten-word telegram, either. It was thirty words—think of that, Dear Mad'm——"

"Twenty-nine," Dearsir interrupted. Up'nUp glanced at him impatiently.

"OK, twenty-nine, then. Anyway, it said he's bringing the president and the chief engineer of the World Mining Company of New York to see our mining claims tomorrow—be here for lunch. So you see, everything's all set."

"I smell a fish in this deal," Dearsir put in. "Mr. Morse just said—"

Up'nUp turned on him. "Dammit, Dearsir, don't go upsetting Dear Mad'm. We all know that big mining promoters like Mr. Morse don't go sending twenty-nine-word telegrams to people unless a sale is as good as made, all but signing the papers. Now let's get busy and divide the dough."

Up'nUp pulled my writing tablet off the shelf and took my fountain pen from a catchall on the table.

"Let's see. Thirty thousand would be about right for you, Dearsir, being you're the biggest claim owner. Twenty for me, being I'm the second biggest. Ten for you, Dear Mad'm, being as you're on the ground and have shown more interest than the others, paid for your assessment work and the like. The others left their assessment work for me and Dearsir to do and never paid us a cent for it."

"I trust," said Dearsir with what for him was heavy-handed

sarcasm, "that you'll wait to make the final division until we have consulted with our other partners—and the mere formality of our being paid the cash has been completed."

This made only the slightest impression on me and was completely lost as far as Up'nUp was concerned. He was delirious with joyful excitement, already felt his pockets stuffed with folding money. As for me, it was all too much, the sums of money too big for me to realize. I thought maybe I had misunderstood him.

"You mean—you really mean—ten thousand dollars for *me?*"

"Exactly."

"Just like my thirty thousand," said Dearsir. "Which I don't have yet. Or doesn't that interest you two?"

"Pay no attention to him, Dear Mad'm. He just naturally looks on the dark side. Plan how you will spend your money and rest easy. I'm going to set aside five thousand right this minute for my boy's education."

"But he's only a month—or is it five weeks—old!"

"Makes no difference, Dear Mad'm. They begin educating them young these days. My boy may be one of those prodigies you've read about—like being able to add eight columns of figures in his head, or telling you right off the bat how old Julius Caesar was when Marcus Aurelius stabbed him."

"No, Up'nUp, it was Mark Antony who——" This remark, which I didn't bother to finish, was no more than reflex action on my part. Nobody, least of all I, cared who finished off Caesar. It took Dearsir to bring us back to the consideration of more immediate and practical matters.

"Mr. Morse and the two big shots he's bringing with him will be here about noon tomorrow—the telegram said so. The least we can do is to have a big feed ready for them."

"By the great horn spoon!" Up'nUp shouted, pushing back his chair and letting out a war whoop. "We'll give 'em a party.

We'll show them city fellers! Let's have steak and mushrooms, lobster salad—champagne——"

"How'll we get 'em?" Dearsir said, with a flash of annoyance. "First place, we don't have money for that sort of thing. Second place, we probably couldn't get any of them except steak at Happy Camp, even if we had time to go there for them, which we haven't. Third place, who's to cook such fancy victuals?"

"Dear Mad'm, of course. You'd do that much for us, wouldn't you?"

"Of course. But I think we'd better have a simple luncheon —we'll have to use what we have on hand, as Dearsir says."

"Simple? With a mining promoter and two New York big shots coming? Aw, gee—"

"Well, maybe it could be a little on the fancy side," Dearsir said cautiously. "I could maybe catch a nice fat steelhead early tomorrow morning. Dear Mad'm could bake it with stuffing and tomato sauce. Now let's see—there's plenty of vegetables—cabbage and tomatoes. How about a tomato salad?" He turned to me. I nodded. "Well, that ought to be enough."

"What?" yelled Up'nUp. "No dessert? What kind of lunch is that for big mining men who are going to write us a check for seventy-five thousand dollars?"

"You've got something there," Dearsir said. "Well, I've an idea—Dear Mad'm can bring down two jars of her blackcap raspberries and make a big pie."

"That ought to do it," said Up'nUp, his good humor restored. "Don't sound bad at all. And we've got a half-dozen bottles of ginger ale—that ain't champagne, but—"

"Let's go." Dearsir stood up. "We better give Dear Mad'm a chance to rest. She's going to be busy tomorrow."

"You be thinking up some nice horse doovers or something," said Up'nUp jauntily in parting.

When I was sure they were out of hearing, I got out of my chair and slammed the door. I was thoroughly angry. Those boys! Not even asking me if I could cook the fancy meal they planned—just telling me. For all I cared, I told myself firmly, they could give the visitors sliced salami, pretzels and beer, of which I knew they had plenty.

I set up Contraption and drowsily cold-creamed my wrinkles. All this talk about money—big money. I had never in my life had ten thousand dollars in one lump to spend as I pleased. It wasn't enough to make some of my fancier dreams come true—it was too much for others—there'd be bothersome small sums left over . . .

Suddenly I was too tired to think about it any more—and fell asleep in my old rocking chair. I didn't stay asleep very long, but woke up right in the middle of cooking a wonderful meal for the boys' party. Roast turkey, hearts of artichoke salad with avocado dressing. Frozen eggnog. Angel cake.

Pity is, it was all a dream.

Thinking more clearly after my brief nap, I knew I couldn't let the boys down, but would pitch in and give them the very best meal I could. Undressing, I crept into bed and turned the kerosene lamp wick down until the flame died.

"Are you there, Vicki?" I asked. Vicki flapped her tail on the floor under my bed. All was well. Let tomorrow bring what it might. I went to sleep.

Next morning, lying snugly in my bed long after Tom's mail truck had buzzed past in the direction of Orleans, I heard the boys' jalopy come to a rattling halt at the foot of my trail. I sprang out of bed—in a manner of speaking. Actually, I pushed back the blankets, dragged myself to a sitting position, threw my legs stiffly over the side of the bed, reached for my old blue robe—and got to the door just in time to shove Contraption aside into a heap, open the door and peer sleepily into Up'nUp's excited face.

"I thought I'd better come and get you," he said. "Come on —step lively, Dear Mad'm."

"But I'm not dressed—I haven't had breakfast yet—what's the rush at this unearthly hour?"

"There's nothing unearthly about it! Cooking fancy food takes time. Dearsir has already caught one of the finest fish you ever saw. It's cleaned, ready for the stuffin'. Better get your things together. Where's them blackcap raspberries?"

"They're in the cellar," I said shortly. I never did take kindly to being bossed. "You'll give me time to get dressed, I hope?"

"Sure, I will. But don't dawdle. Dearsir's mixing pancakes for our breakfast."

Well, that last item was something. Dearsir's pancakes were always something to cheer the heart. I didn't dawdle. Just before I left to go down to the car I snatched up an apron, a handful of clean dish towels, some paper napkins and a powder puff; equipment no woman can afford to be without when going to a man's apartment.

Arriving at Bent Pine, I found Dearsir peering at himself in a mirror on the wall no bigger than a post card. He took umbrage at my quizzical glances.

"There is nothing wrong with this mirror, Dear Mad'm. This is a very good mirror—or was before it got cracked." He lathered his face vigorously.

"Really? Just the same, I don't think I could use that mirror."

"Well, thank God you don't have to. I'd hate to see you trying to shave."

"What are we talking about, Dearsir? I thought we were talking about a certain, specific mirror."

"I'd rather not talk about this mirror any more, if you don't mind," he said bitterly. "I can't be a gentleman and talk about this mirror when I'm shaving, and I don't like to cuss in the

presence of a lady. You're right, Dear Mad'm. This is one hell
of a mirror."

"Trouble is," Up'nUp observed, "his dull old razor is pulling his whiskers. I wish he'd hone it. But he won't—and he
won't let me. And I have to use it when he's through. Anyway, who wants to see himself when he's shaving his mug?"

It seemed best to change the subject. After all, shaving was
their problem—let them solve it. I had troubles of my own.
Right now I was hungry.

"What about those pancakes I was led to believe were waiting for me?" I asked, sniffing. All I could smell was coffee.

"Cook her a stack," Dearsir directed, making faces at what
he could see of himself. "The dough's all mixed, in that bowl
on the table." Then after another spot was scraped, "Fry her
some bacon and an egg, too. We don't want her conking out
on us this morning."

While we were eating the fabulously light and tender pancakes, I suddenly remembered having noticed my cougar
hide as I came down the roadway, still fastened to the wall of
the cabin.

"Up'nUp," I said, "what about my rug? I wish you'd—"

"It'll be ready one of these days, like I told you," he said.
"Don't you worry. Takes time to do it right."

I couldn't see why it took him so long to dry out the skin
so I could put it on my floor. But I hate a nagging woman, so
kept quiet. Finishing the last of my hot cakes, I stood up, tied
on my apron, and was ready.

"Everything's there on the drainboard," Up'nUp said.

I took careful inventory. "No salad dressing," I announced.

"Oh, gosh!" Up'nUp exclaimed. "We don't have any. What
about you?"

"I don't have any, either."

"What do you need to make it?" Dearsir asked.

"Besides what I see here, oil and vinegar."

Up'nUp dragged a chair over, climbed up and began to fumble around on a high shelf.

"What you looking for?" Dearsir demanded.

"There used to be a bottle of sour wine up here—and part of a bottle of castor oil——"

"Of all the—castor oil! *Get down!*" thundered Dearsir. Up'nUp got down, looking hurt.

"I was only trying to help," he muttered.

"One of you go down to my cabin and bring me a bottle of salad oil and one of vinegar. They're on the kitchen shelf by the stove."

Up'nUp stamped indignantly out and I went to work.

By eleven-thirty everything was ready—the baked fish beautifully browned, with rich sauce bubbling around it; the pie oozing thick purple juice; the vegetables tender; the salad chilling in the cooler outside. The boys were in the bedroom putting on their hiking togs. There came a knock at the door. I answered it, my heart beating at trip-hammer speed. Could it be one of the big shots?

It was.

"Good morning, Madam," he said. "My name is Ford—Martin Ford, president of the World Mining Company. Mr. Morse sent you a telegram about me, I believe. He and Mr. Richardson, my associate, are in a car up on the road. I am looking for the owners of the placer mining property. Mr. Morse tells me it is a rather promising prospect."

Prospect, indeed! I thought. Talking like that about the boys' mine.

"Yes sir," I said. "The men will be out in just a moment. Won't you come in?"

"No, thank you," he said courteously. "We're in something of a hurry. We want to get some of the fine fishing we've heard about before mid-afternoon. Just now, we'd like to go up to the diggings for a quick look as soon as possible."

I felt as if someone had hit me in the chest. This man wasn't interested in buying our claims. He was up here to fish for steelhead. All the rest had been dreamed up by that promoter, Morse. Some people might call this woman's intuition. To me, it was just plain common sense.

Dearsir and Up'nUp came out of the bedroom. There was a jumble of greetings between the three men. I had no chance to tell the boys what I thought of the whole thing. They all started out the door. How could I warn Dearsir and Up'nUp ——let them down easy?

"You and your friends will be back to have lunch with us, of course, Mr. Ford," I said, as if the matter were all settled.

"Thank you," he said absently, "but I think not. We brought sandwiches with us. We can eat them on the bank of the river where we are going to fish. We'll take a brief survey of the diggings and be on our way."

Dearsir turned toward me with a startled look. Up'nUp stopped in his tracks.

"Go on, go on," I said urgently, having succeeded too well, with an unconscious assist from the president of the World Mining Company, in getting my point over. "Don't keep Mr. Ford and the other gentlemen waiting." I practically pushed them out the door.

But hope dies hard. Maybe, I thought when I was alone, when Mr. Ford sees the mine and all the boys have done there, when he looks at the receipts from the mint, which I knew Dearsir had in his pocket, showing how much gold the boys had taken out, he might—just might—buy the claims, after all. I put another stick of wood in the stove and dispiritedly surveyed my preparations for giving the big shots a luncheon they would long remember.

An hour later the boys came into the cabin. Up'nUp tossed

his hat up to catch on a peg on the wall. Dearsir sat down on a bench. Neither one looked particularly cast down. Could it be possible . . .

"They didn't buy the claims," Dearsir said. "Far as I could make out, Ford and his sidekick, Richardson, never had any intention of buying them. The whole thing was an excuse they cooked up to get Morse to bring them up here, show them a good place to fish. Now we can settle down to another ten years of peace and quiet."

Did I detect a note of relief in his voice? I certainly did.

"Was that Morse mad!" chortled Up'nUp. "It was worth the whole show to see a mining promoter taken for a ride. When you get right down to brass tacks, I don't want to sell the claims, anyway. What for? What'd I do then? Just buy some more— Ain't that right, Dearsir?"

"Dead right. We're nothing but independent, small-time Little Giant miners at heart, I reckon." He turned to me. "But I'm right sorry for your sake that the deal fell through."

"Don't you worry about me," I said. "I don't know anything more upsetting to an old woman like me than ten thousand dollars you can't decide how to spend. Peace and quiet—and our independence—that's what we want. And thanks to our fishing enthusiasts, we know it. A lot of people never find it out. Now—I'm hungry. Aren't you?"

"Gosh, yes!" Up'nUp scrambled to his place at the table. "Bring on the food, Dear Mad'm!"

We had a wonderful luncheon, liberally seasoned with contentment.

Eighteen

———◆◆◆———

THE days and nights grew steadily colder with the advancing season. Scarlet and yellow leaves fell, leaving bare branches outlined against the green of firs and pines, or against the sky, blue most of the time, occasionally gray with clouds. My chrysanthemums, blackened by frost, had to be cleared away. Light snows fell, melted quickly, and were gone. The boys filled my woodshed to bursting with split oak and fir. All day a fire crackled and glowed in the big old stove that long ago had been the pride of some woman's heart. I liked to imagine that it came around the horn in one of those old sailing vessels, then was brought up to this country on mule-back over the faintest of trails, or no trail at all. A fine, dignified stove, for all its molded curlicues, and it kept Vicki and me warm and snug.

By the last of November most of the wildflower seed pods had burst, their contents sifting down through the loose carpet of dry pine needles and drifting brown leaves, out of reach of my friends, the birds. How or where they found food I did not know, but many remained, though they must often have been hungry. I tied scraps of fat to the leafless branches of the little peach and apricot trees and scattered crumbs on the bare ground in my yard. Dozens of little birds, some brightly colored, some a modest gray, came to feast on this bounty. They gave me hours of entertainment as I watched their dartings and flittings from my kitchen window. Then there were the timid quail that used their wings only when startled. They came walking daintily from the low bushes, chirping their low, musical call. For these trim, lovely birds I kept something special—a bag of crushed barley. This they loved, filling their crops eagerly with the rich grain.

The boys gathered the last of the vegetables in the Bent Pine garden and stored them in the tool house, carefully protected by old newspapers and gunny sacks so they wouldn't freeze. A great deal of covering wasn't required. Our weather along the Klamath was never severe. Dearsir and Up'nUp, in their usual generous fashion, told me that I was to share in this harvest, when and however much I wished. There was, in fact, much more than we could possibly use. But if I knew those boys, they'd give much of it away before the products of next spring's garden would be ready to eat.

Days slipped by until one morning the calendar announced that the twentieth of December had come—it was almost Christmas. I looked out my kitchen window and thought I had never seen a more beautiful day—all blue and gold and green. Weeks before, I had refused to leave my little cabin to spend a proper Christmas out in the world with my family— where beautiful trees were turned into a framework to hold blazing lights and glittering gimcracks. Very pretty they were, too, but I preferred to stay where the trees would keep on growing after Christmas, just as they had done before. Some called me stubborn, others used the words, "slightly unbalanced." Anyone who wanted to stay away from the conventional joys of Christmas—well, it just wasn't natural.

But I felt very well satisfied as I stood looking out that window. Across the River mighty evergreens clothed the mountain slopes that lifted their heights to meet the sky.

What could be more satisfying—except for me to be outside, a part of this wonder world? I decided I would go to Bent Pine to get a head of cabbage and half a dozen eggs, even though I knew the boys were not there. They had gone to Happy Camp for a supply of staple groceries for themselves and to fill my order for, among other things, beef, suet, raisins, spices and so on for the mince pie I was to make for our Christmas dinner.

I pulled on my heavy tweed coat—and there was Vicki fanning my legs with her plumy tail, making whimpering sounds of joy. With my little Iver Johnson pistol tucked in my canvas vegetable sack, Vicki and I set out for the Bent Pine claim. As we went down the short stretch of private road leading to the boys' cabin, I stopped to peer into the shadowy tool house. I had been there several times, even made one brief effort at straightening it up, but had desisted before making any appreciable impression on its shocking disorder. But now was my chance. Dearsir and Up'nUp wouldn't be back before dark. This was going to be a joy. And Dearsir would be so grateful.

The first task was to get what looked like a small barbecue grill out of the way. It wasn't too heavy, but offered considerable resistance as it stood on four spraddled iron legs. After much pulling and hauling, I managed to shove it against the rear wall, thereby covering myself with charcoal dust.

What to do next was a problem. But a nail keg standing near the workbench gave me an idea. I gathered up nails of every kind—straight, bent, and rusted, large and small, and dropped them into the keg. At one end of the bench I found a half dozen or so little boxes labeled "Hungarian Nails." What in the world, I wondered, would anyone want of Hungarian nails. They, too, went into the keg. By this time it was level-full.

Then I wrestled the empty cartons around, piled them in

neat stacks, sorted out the contents of other cartons, put old boots in one pile, various items of clothing in another, all of which seemed past any hope of usefulness. Stuffing these into boxes, I shoved the boxes far back under the workbench.

Hours went by and I seemed to be making some progress. But my arms began to ache and my knees to wobble from standing so long. I threw an old blanket over the nail keg and sat down on it. With great satisfaction I thought of telling Dearsir that my cleaning up of the tool house would be my Christmas gift to him; and a very practical sort that would be sure to please him. On Sunday, when the boys did not go to the mine, they never found time for a cleaning job like this. They always had a big washing to do, swamping out the cabin, cleaning the nannies' barn on the hill across the road, filling the mangers with hay—well, anyway, they called it their rest day.

I knew I mustn't sit too long patting myself on the back, so I went at the bench again, my back to the wide-open door. When I started the job the day had been all before me. And I didn't realize it was all behind me until a crisp little breeze lifted my skirt and sent a chill up my tired legs. I dropped a handful of small hammers and looked out to see a veil of falling snow. As I looked it changed to a downfall of feathers from a giant feather bed. The strange gloom that had settled over the outside world frightened me. I ran for the cabin, Vicki at my heels. We were almost there when I saw that my cougar skin was gone from the wall. That meant it must be thoroughly dry. Then why hadn't Up'nUp given it to me? It hurt me that he hadn't—because of sheer carelessness, I was sure—given me my rug. I really needed it, now that cold weather had come. Should I speak to him again about it—jog his memory? No, I would not! He could just take his own good time . . .

Inside the cabin the air was stale, smelling of old tobacco

smoke and sundry wet garments hung along the wall to dry. I dropped into a chair and comforted myself with the thought that the boys would be showing up before long and take me and my groceries down to my cabin. Meantime, I would start a fire in the rusty stove, get the chill out of my bones, and have the cabin warm for them when they came.

Dearsir's kindling box was full of thinly split sticks, each seemingly exactly like every other stick, and neatly arranged. I hated to disturb this mathematic accuracy, but a fire must be built and kindling is nothing to get sentimental about. I chose an old newspaper, carefully selected as to date, so I would not burn a recent one, took a handful of the kindling and a few sticks of wood from a pile as neatly arranged as the kindling. I put these in the fire-box of the stove, then looked about for a match.

I knew that matches were absolutely necessary to two pipe-smoking men, but for the life of me, I couldn't see a match anywhere. Shaking with cold, I started a determined inch-by-inch search for matches. After running my fingers over sundry shelves, books, tobacco cans and other oddments, I gave up. No matches. Maybe the boys had used all they had and planned to get more in Happy Camp. So I was without a fire and couldn't even light the lamp.

Vicki, the mind reader, was trembling at my side and I began to tremble myself, thinking what might be ahead of me. A night of freezing cold and inky darkness—if the boys didn't show up. It was black night outside by this time and I knew it would be folly for me to try to make my way back to my cabin.

Hunger was gnawing at my vitals—whatever they are. A breakfast of toast and coffee isn't very sustaining and I had put in several hours of unremitting toil in that tool house. Earlier, I had taken note of some cold beans in a kettle on the stove with an iron spoon sticking out of them. So a cold-bean supper it would be. How an empty stomach can make a pig of a usually fastidious woman is no longer a marvel to me. I didn't stop eating until the spoon hit the bottom of the kettle.

Time passed. I gave up expecting Dearsir and Up'nUp that night and began worrying about why they hadn't come home. Maybe something had happened to them on the mountain road that twisted its precarious length between Happy Camp and the Bent Pine cabin. Maybe the car had slipped over the edge, pitched down a precipice and now lay, the boys trapped inside, at the bottom of the Klamath River. Maybe a great rock, bounding down the mountainside, had smashed the car. Maybe a landslide—I stopped myself sharply. I was doing the boys no good, or myself either. More probably they had stayed at Happy Camp to see a picture show, then decided it would be safer to drive back next morning.

By this time the cold had reached my very bones. I lay down on the bunk, pulled the top blankets about me and huddled into them. I fell asleep—but not for long. Soon Vicki came nuzzling under the blankets and whimpering in my ear, telling me she was cold and lonely. So was I. In desperation, I turned the blankets back until I came to white blanket-sheets. I had minor compunctions about getting in between them, for I was fully dressed, even to my shoes.

At this point I realized that it was almost as bright as day in the cabin. Moonlight streamed across the floor, the whitest, brightest moonlight I had ever seen. Going to the window, I looked across the tossing river to the mountain that rose sharply from the other bank. Every trace of clouds had gone. In the short time I had been asleep the forest had been completely changed by the snow. The close-set trees had become tall, pointed white tents outlined along the mountain top against an indigo sky. My word, it was cold.

I took a newspaper off the shelf, wrapped it around my

shoes, squirmed between the white blanket-sheets and pulled the covers over my head. Before I had time to draw a breath of satisfaction Vicki scrambled over the foot of the bunk. A moment later she had her head tucked into the hollow of my back. "Happy dreams," I said to Vicki, and was out of this world.

It may have been a passing car returning from an all-night dance at Happy Camp, or it may have been my own conscience that woke me. I scrambled out of my warm nest and Vicki and I hit the floor together. The sun shone, Dearsir's clock told me it was fifteen minutes before eight. Did I hear the rattle of Up'nUp's old jalopy? Good heavens! I didn't want the boys to know I had been so frightened that I had spent the night at their cabin. Hurriedly I arranged the tumbled blankets on Dearsir's bed. There was the big iron spoon on the table, sticky with beans. I stumbled over Vicki, dashed to the sink with it. One swipe with the dish rag and another dash back to the stove. Thank heaven I had remembered to put the giant spoon back in its place, where it would tell no tales.

The rattling car passed on down the road. More than one good citizen drove a jalopy in this far country, but I was taking no chances. I pulled on my heavy coat, caught up my little canvas bag—never mind about vegetables now—and with Vicki in front of me, hurried up to the road. There was no snow under the trees and in the road it had been churned into muddy slush by the passing car. Now if I could keep up this pace I would be around the first curve before the boys hove in sight. I was wheezing by this time and fearful of meeting some traveler who'd lift an eyebrow at meeting a woman coming away from the boys' cabin at this hour of the morning. That thought started me on the run until I reached the bars at the bottom of the steep trail that led to my cabin. I'd made it! The boys' reputations were saved.

I made a fire in the kitchen stove and soon the cabin was warm and cheerful, filled with the smell of coffee, frying bacon, and toast. I fed Vicki and she lay at my feet, thumping her beautiful tail on the floor in appreciation. I straightened up the cabin and waited impatiently for the boys to show up with the makings of my Christmas pie. Cars passed now and then on the road below my cabin, so I was no longer worried. If misfortune had befallen Dearsir and Up'nUp I would have heard about it by now. But I was lonely without them. The boys had come to mean a great deal to me. They gave me comradeship—the kind that keeps a woman like me from slipping into the limbo of old age.

It wasn't long until I heard Dearsir and Up'nUp climbing my trail. Vicki ran to the door. I hailed them over Vicki's joyful barking.

"Good morning! Good morning!" I called, determined not to say anything that would reveal the fact that I knew they had not come home last night.

"Good morning," Dearsir said stiffly. He set the box he was carrying on the table, turned, went out the door and up the trail that led to the diggings. Up'nUp started to follow, but I held him back by one arm.

"Wait a minute," I said. "Why does Dearsir act so glum?"

He shuffled his feet and looked up the path after the rapidly disappearing Dearsir.

"Tell me," I insisted.

"Well, damn it," he began, "why did you stay there all night, anyway?"

"Me? Stay where all night—"

"Yes, you! Don't deny it." He bent over the box of groceries and pulled out what was undeniably my handkerchief. "Dearsir found this on the floor by his bed. And how about the kindling and wood—and Dearsir's *Siskiyou News* he was saving—all stuffed into the fire box?" Up'nUp would have been glaring if he could have managed it with his big blue eyes.

"And we'd *like* to know why you didn't touch it off instead of crawling into Dearsir's bed to keep warm."

"I—I couldn't find a match," I stammered.

"You couldn't have used your eyes, Dear Mad'm. They were on the plate right over the stove—a whole box of 'em."

I began to feel annoyed.

"You're trying to fool me," I said. "There was no plate anywhere about the stove. I looked over every inch of space around there."

"You know, Dear Mad'm, I think you're trying to fool *me*. No cabin can be built without a plate. The ends of all the rafters rest on it. Just put that in your notebook."

"Oh, you mean the square piece of timber—"

"I mean the plate."

"Oh, all right—the plate, then. I didn't look there. Now you tell me what's the matter with Dearsir. He couldn't really be miffed because I stayed all night in your cabin."

"Dear Mad'm, the truth is, he is more than miffed, he's plain hot under the collar—but not at your staying in the cabin. It's because you messed around the tool house. This morning when he went out there to get his Hungarian nails, he couldn't find hide nor hair of them—nor a lot of other things, either. He has to have Hungarian nails in this kind of weather. You can't climb trails like we got this morning without nails in the soles of your boots—and damn it all! He couldn't find a nail of any kind, let alone Hungarian, and they're the ones that work the best. You'd swept that workbench clean, so help me God!"

He shook my hand from his arm and bolted through the doorway. Once in the clear, he called back to me, "You'll find the makin's for the mince pie in the box!" and was off on his long-legged stride up the mountain.

That was a busy day for me and I didn't have time to worry over Dearsir's attitude toward my well-intentioned activities at Bent Pine. I'd tell him that I'd taken good care of his Hungarian nails—he'd find every one in the keg—and all would be well between us again. He flared up easily, but he never stayed angry very long.

Going through the box of groceries, I found everything I had asked the boys to get for the mince pie—even suet—except meat. No pie! I thought dismally. Then I remembered the venison jerky Nora and I had made months ago. Well, why not use that? I pounded some of it into a coarse sort of pemmican and put it to soak. I chopped citron and suet, cut apples in tiny pieces, measured spices, seeded raisins.

By afternoon the mincemeat was made, spooned into a jar and set on the shelf to ripen until Christmas day. I made a big potful of coffee, hoping the boys would stop in on their way home from the diggings. They did.

I felt I had to make things right with Dearsir, and started by pouring him a cup of steaming coffee.

"I'm sorry about the tool house and—and the nails," I stammered.

"I've always heard that a woman's work is in her home." Dearsir interrupted my halting apology with so much asperity that all my repentance and humility flew out the door. I could have turned him over my knee and spanked him—if, of course, he had been thirty years younger.

"You needn't take that tone with me—" I began hotly.

"Haw!" Up'nUp said, and ducked out the door, leaving his coffee to get cold. If Dearsir and I were going to quarrel, he definitely wasn't having any.

Dearsir sampled his coffee, set the cup down.

"If you don't mind, Dear Mad'm," he said, "please tell me where you hid my six boxes of Hungarian nails."

"Why, they're in the nail keg, of course. And I didn't hide them, I just put them where they belonged. If you'd used the sense God gave you and lifted the blanket I threw over the keg so I could sit down—"

"Hm-m-m-m," he said. "So that's why I couldn't even find

the keg." I saw the twinkle in his nice gray eyes. In spite of his occasional crustiness and snapping-turtle sort of remarks, I defy any woman to hang onto her wrath in the face of that friendly twinkle. I knew the subject was buried forever and that we were friends again. But I learned a lesson—very valuable at my time of life. Never disturb a bachelor's bed; never touch even one of his old newspapers; and never, *never* clean up his tool house.

"Up'nUp says he's going to spend Christmas with Nora and the baby in Yreka," Dearsir said.

I nodded. "Of course. We might have known he'd want to do that. Then there'll just be you and me for Christmas dinner."

"Well, Dear Mad'm—if you don't mind, I'd like to ask a man I know in Happy Camp."

"Of course I don't mind. Who is he?"

"Kirk Hubert is his name. He's the construction boss on that motel some company is building just the other side of Happy Camp. He has a wife and two children—they live in San Diego—and he's stuck up here on this job. Can't get home for the holidays. He seemed pretty unhappy about it, so I thought—"

"By all means, go ahead and ask him."

"To tell you the truth, I already have," he grinned. "I was sure it would be all right with you."

"Why don't we ask Frenchy, too?" I said on a sudden impulse.

"All right, I will. But won't you be too crowded, Dear Mad'm?"

"Sure. We all will," I said recklessly. "But who cares about a little thing like that on Christmas Day?"

"Not you, anyway. The day before Christmas I'll take Up'nUp to Happy Camp and he can get a bus from there to Yreka. I'll bring back the turkey and the rest of the fixin's. Kirk will drive down Christmas morning."

Dearsir finished his coffee and said goodbye. I stood at the kitchen window, watching him go down the trail to the bars, then turn up the road toward Bent Pine. Not until then did I begin to think how I would seat four people at my small kitchen table—especially when I had only three chairs —and how I would stretch my few dishes so there would be enough to go around. And the thought of the man from San Diego began to trouble me, too. What would he think of my cabin, of a Christmas dinner served on thick, common dishes, some of them chipped? Well, I should have thought of that sooner . . .

Then it was the day before Christmas. I had no time to think of all the other "days before Christmas" that had, happily, sorrowfully, or just drudgingly, gone over my head. The making of the crust for the mince pie, the scramble in the cellar for old cracked cups, saucers, plates, to fill out the collection of antiques in my cupboard . . . as for the extra seat, I knew Dearsir could manage on an upturned orange crate. But this Kirk Hubert—this city man— I felt a little shy of him. There had been many years when I was unexcited by city men—they being the only kind I knew. I hoped he would not come all togged out in an elegant custom-made suit and put Frenchy to shame.

That evening—and Christmas Eve it was—Dearsir stomped into my kitchen carrying a huge carton.

"Here's the bird," he announced cheerfully. "All plucked and drawn, ready for the oven." He set the box down. "Where'll I hang it, Dear Mad'm? Not in the cellar—too many civet cats around. The woodshed's no good—a nighthawk might get in and make a meal off it. We'll have to hang it in your bedroom—I see no other place."

By this time he had pulled the turkey out of the box. It was quite a sight; big, white, its neck neatly wrapped in paper. He held it up by its long legs and went into the other room. I followed and watched him hang the enormous bird directly over my bed, using the pulley and wire that had held my bedding aloft that first night I returned to the cabin

after a long absence. Dearsir was so pleased with his solution of the problem that I didn't protest. After all, what else was there to do? I knew I was in for a night with a gleaming white carcass gamboling and gobbling through my dreams.

His work done, and completely to his satisfaction, I might add, Dearsir went back to Bent Pine. I had one more chore to attend to before I could crawl into bed. I had to unpack the groceries still in the big box that had also held the turkey, and get it out of the kitchen so I wouldn't have to face that job in the morning when there'd be so much else to do. I found everything I had ordered and put the bottles and packages on the shelf. Then I discovered there was another layer of something in the box, neatly covered with white tissue paper.

What's this? I thought, feeling a flutter of excitement, and pulled the paper away. There lay three boxes, very festive-looking in gay wrappings and bows of red ribbon. I opened them in a childish daze of suspense and surprise. There was a little card in each one, with "From Dearsir" written on it in the impersonal handwriting of some clerk. In one there was a pair of lovely furry bedroom slippers— he knew my old ones were worn to a frazzle—in another, good-looking stationery with the initial "P" engraved on it, and the last box held my favorite candy, chocolate-covered cherries.

I was about to carry the carton outside when I saw another package, so bulky that it covered the bottom of the box. This was not done up in city style as Dearsir's boxes had been, but was crookedly wrapped in a copy of the *Siskiyou News* and tied with two kinds of string. There was no card to identify the sender.

Wonderingly I lifted it out, tore off the newspaper. Out tumbled the cougar skin; thick, soft, pliable, backed with heavy green felt. It had been sent to San Francisco for that last professional touch which Up'nUp could not give it. So that was why he hadn't given it to me before.

Those two wonderful boys. I wiped my eyes, blew my nose, and crept into bed.

Nineteen

IT MAY have been a dream featuring the white carcass of
the turkey hanging from the ceiling, or it may have been
the cold that woke me just as the first rays of the sun
came shooting across the River from the opposite mountain-
top. A strange, unreal light filled the room. I recognized it
at once as sunshine reflected from snow. Springing up, I
pulled my old blue robe about me, pulled on my scuffed
bedroom slippers and opened the front door. A thick layer
of sparkling crystals blanketed everything. This was no thin
snow such as we had had before, but snow that turned rocks
and bushes into smooth mounds, weighted down tree
branches, gave a muffled quality to the deep-toned voice of
the River.

Only yesterday I had congratulated myself on being out
of the holiday turmoil, the synthetically created commercial
bustle of the cities that makes mature people wearily pes-
simistic and regretful of the passing of other and simpler
days. But now, suddenly and quite unreasonably, I felt sorry
for myself, far away from all but the mildest Christmas
symbols, Christmas gaiety, marooned in the Siskiyou Mountains, nostalgically aware of all I was missing—all that now
seemed warm and dear . . . a change of heart no doubt

brought on by the Christmas-card scene at which I was looking.

I closed the door, started a fire in the stove. The Christmas spirit had passed me by. I had heard no happy voices of children, no Christmas carols, seen no wreaths in lighted windows. Suddenly something dragged me out of this sentimental bog of self-pity.

A flock of snowbirds wheeled past my kitchen window, missing the glass by inches. I had forgotten their morning crumbs and they took this way of reminding me. Putting down the coffeepot, I reached for a small box of crackers. This morning, I thought, I'll give the little wild things a fine Christmas breakfast.

I gathered up other items—raisins and shreds of suet left over from the mince pie, an apple peeled and threaded on a string, a cupful of crushed barley for my especially beloved quail. Quietly removing Contraption so as not to startle my visitors, I opened the door and stepped outside. Dozens of hungry little creatures came fluttering and twittering about me. Tiny blue birds, gray birds with plum-colored topknots, birds with yellow breasts, brilliant red-headed fellows, bossy and spiteful—and, hovering close to the ground, a few timid mountain quail. My spirits, so low a few minutes before, lifted and soared.

Did any human being ever have a more cheerful Christmas greeting? I impaled the suet on twigs of trees, spread the raisins on a board wedged flat between the bare limbs of a peach tree, hung the apple by its string, scattered cracker crumbs and crushed barley with a prodigal hand, until there was no more.

That done, I broke off an armful of holly oak that grew in a fringe along the bank, shook the snow from the branches and took my treasure trove into the cabin. My thin old slippers were soaked, my hands stiff and red from the cold, but I was full of newborn Christmas spirit. Kicking off the shapeless, sodden slippers, I put on the luxurious ones Dearsir had given me, then shaped the holly oak branches into wreaths. They were more angular than round and had a weatherbeaten air that sort of fitted into the general effect of my cabin. I hung them in the windows, then added the red-ribbon bows that had come on Dearsir's presents to me. That last touch gave them the proper holiday look.

I used every scrap of holly oak left over from the wreaths to frame my foggy old mirror and the map of the United States that added color and interest to one bedroom wall. Standing in the door to study the effect, I was not quite satisfied. A madrone branch clustered thick with bright orange berries—how that would brighten up the cabin! But though madrones grew along my trail, the berries hung fifty feet above my head. I'd have to be content with what I had.

Time slipped away, as it so often does with me. Suddenly it was ten o'clock. Dearsir and his guest—Kirk something-or-other—might show up at any minute, and I hadn't made my bed, dressed myself properly, or got the turkey down from its hook.

I hurriedly put on my clothes and made the bed. Then I started to retrieve the turkey. In a few minutes exhaustion overtook me from pulling at that dratted turkey's legs. I dropped on the bed, puffing for breath. Ever since I was seventy I have known better than to hurry. But I keep on doing it.

Vicki began to bark joyously. I had to move fast, or in another minute Dearsir would be helping me off the bed and standing me on my feet to face his friend from San Diego. I rose, pushed my hair out of my eyes, made an effort to appear dignified and poised, as a hostess should. But it was no use. The two men stepped inside the front door. The city man apparently did not see me as an individual, but as part of a very funny sight that included a turkey's cadaver hanging by its feet from the ceiling. He shouted with laughter, threw off his handsome overcoat, and began to loosen the wire that held aloft the *pièce de résistance* of our Christmas dinner.

In less than a minute the plump white bird lay sprawled on the kitchen table. Now that there was time for introductions, none were needed. I was calling the stranger Kirk and he —following Dearsir's example—was calling me Dear Mad'm, as if we had known each other for years. Kirk was quite a young fellow—somewhere between forty and forty-five, I guessed—big, good-looking in a rugged sort of way. He wore his city clothes well and overflowed with exuberant good humor. He seemed not to know how to speak except at the top of his lungs.

So many things can happen in the time it takes to reach for an apron, pick up a hairpin, use it to fasten back a stray lock. While I was engaged in these simple acts, Dearsir shoved three sticks of wood into the stove, Kirk snatched a dish towel off the rack, tucked it into his belt apron-wise, severed the feet of the turkey and had the bird in a baking pan.

"Where's your stuffing?" he shouted jovially as I stood aghast in the kitchen door.

"Why—why, I haven't made it yet."

"Just give me what it takes, Dear Mad'm, and I'll mix it."

What assurance, I thought indignantly, but I obeyed him, assembling dry bread, a half-pound of sausage, celery, salt, pepper and sage. Then I stood back and marveled at Kirk's expert performance. This man knew what he was doing.

"Guess you can tell I'm a married man." His laughter shook the kitchen. "My wife broke me to kitchen harness before we'd been married a month. Good thing, too. When she isn't feeling well, or has gone visiting, I can feed the kids as well as she can. Take a chair, Dear Mad'm—sit in the doorway so

I won't stumble over you. I'll cook your Christmas dinner —be glad to."

Dearsir looked at me apprehensively. He had bossed me around quite a bit himself—always for my own good, of course—but even he hadn't dared to take such liberties in my kitchen. But somehow it seemed all right for Kirk to act in this fashion. I sat down as I had been told to do, and watched.

It wasn't long until Kirk had the turkey in the oven. Then he went on to plan the rest of the dinner according to his own ideas, and what he found on the kitchen shelves.

"Mashed potatoes," he said thoughtfully, "creamed onions —I see you have plenty—apple, celery and lettuce salad— I'll make French dressing—and—and—by the great horn spoon! Do I see mince pie? No one could ask for a finer dinner than we'll have, Dear Mad'm! Oh, I forgot something."

He dashed into the other room, returned with a paper sack from which he extracted a bottle of sparkling burgundy.

"For you, Dear Mad'm," he said, bowing ceremoniously. "May it add a bit to your Christmas cheer."

"Thank you, Kirk," I said gratefully. "We'll drink a toast to Christmas as we eat dinner. Dearsir, please put it outside to chill."

"Now," Kirk said briskly, "I'll set the table for three."

"Four," I said. "Another guest will be here before long."

"That's going to make things crowded." Kirk frowned, then went on cheerfully, "I suppose I can pull the table out from the wall—manage somehow."

"I hope you won't find it too difficult having him here," I said, very thinly veiling the sarcasm of my words.

"Oh, no, no," Kirk assured me kindly. "I'll manage nicely. Help me shove the table over a bit, will you, Dearsir? Now —a few inches this way—a little more—good!"

Kirk went on with his task of getting dinner ready. Talk,

laughter and good smells filled the cabin. Two hours went by—Kirk reported that the turkey was almost done. Vicki gave her warning yip-yip that meant someone was coming up the trail. Dearsir opened the door and M'sieu Frenchy came in. But this was a changed Frenchy, not the wild, garlic-scented savage I was used to seeing striding along the road. Wonder of wonders, his beard was trimmed and shining clean. A rakish beret perched on his bushy hair, a new bandana encircled his neck. He had squeezed his big body into a black velveteen jacket reminiscent of Beaux Arts days, but below it appeared the jaded old pants he always wore—perhaps he had no others—tucked into heavy knee boots.

I made an attempt to introduce Kirk and Frenchy, but got nowhere. There were shouts of laughter, much beating of each others' backs and a tangle of French and English. Evidently they had met before—in a bar at Happy Camp, I guessed.

"Sit down! Sit down, everybody. Let's eat!" Kirk shouted.

"Pardon," said Frenchy, switching to his Oxford accent. "First, I wish to present Madame with a small memento of Christmas." He produced from behind his back where he had been concealing it all this time, a lovely madrone branch laden with orange berries.

"Oh, thank you, Frenchy!" I exclaimed with delight. "That will put the finishing touch to my decorations. Give it to me."

"But wait, Madame. I have a real present for you—something choice. I made it myself from my mother's prized recipe."

He set a pound coffee can on the table.

"*Pâté de foie gras*," he said reverently.

"Good lord, a pound of it!" Kirk shouted. "Let's have some on crackers for an appetizer right now!"

I shook my head regretfully. "Sorry. No crackers. I fed all I had to the birds. Will toast do?"

Quickly Kirk had bread browning on top of the stove and

was prying the coffee can open. Out came a mysterious and tantalizing odor—exotic, I guess you'd call it. Dearsir turned pale. Kirk spread a generous spoonful of the *pâté de foie gras* on a piece of toast and set his teeth into it. I thought I detected a startled look on his face, accompanied by a fleeting moment of hesitation. If so, they were instantly gone. He turned to Frenchy, chewing zestfully.

"Wonderful! Wonderful!" he mumbled. "But where, Frenchy, did you get goose livers in this country?"

"Non, non, my friend, there are no geese in the Siskiyous. Like much *Pâté de foie gras* in *la belle France,* this is made from good, fat horse liver."

Kirk nodded, took another bite. Dearsir moved unobtrusively toward the front door, his pallor increasing. It was, I saw, time for me to assert myself.

"Thank you, thank you, Frenchy. I prize your gift highly." I picked up the can, put the lid on, pressed it down—tightly. "Dearsir," I called, "will you please take this to the cellar? I hate to seem selfish, but after all, Frenchy gave this to *me,* you know."

Frenchy's beard quivered with pleasure. I saw what I thought to be a look of gratitude in Kirk's eyes. Dearsir grabbed the coffee can, dashed out the back door. Frenchy turned to hang his beret on a nail. Kirk took advantage of the moment to drop his toast and *pâté de foie gras* into the firebox of the stove.

Dearsir came back. Frenchy seated himself expansively. Kirk placed the big, delectable-looking bird on the table, in the roasting pan. There was no platter, as he very well knew by this time. With plates, knives, forks, spoons, cups and saucers, there was no room for anything else on the table. The top of the stove became our buffet, sideboard, serving table, or whatever.

Kirk poured the sparkling burgundy into our thick white

china cups and we drank to the spirit of Christmas everywhere. Then we attacked the delectable food Kirk had prepared. No one could have had a gayer, more altogether satisfying Christmas dinner than we did in that remote and primitive cabin, with the wind in the fir trees and the great Klamath River furnishing organ music to accompany our feast.

The long shadows of late afternoon were creeping up the eastern side of the canyon when we rose from the table. The walls of the little kitchen seemed to have drawn us together in a feeling of comradeship, even affection. What matter that we ate from thick, chipped dishes, had scant elbowroom? We had shared the spirit of Christmas.

Twenty

———◄••••►———

JANUARY is generally the coldest month of the year in the Siskiyous. Sometimes, as in December, we get a few inches of snow down near the River. When that happens we know there has been a deep snowfall higher in the mountains. Only a few hundred feet in elevation will make a difference between a scattering of flakes that soon melt, and six inches to a foot of dry snow at the diggings. At my cabin the temperature during the night often fell ten or fifteen degrees below freezing, but generally the middle of the day was not really cold—just pleasantly crisp.

One morning I woke to find that a light powdering of snow had fallen during the night. After breakfast I thought I would step out into my front yard and see what the world looked like. The thin film of icy crystals on the doorstep was my undoing. My foot slipped. I pitched forward for several running steps, tried frantically to regain my balance. I succeeded—but in the effort I did something to the same leg I had hurt by tripping over a wire nearly nine months before.

Limping into the cabin, I sat down in my creaky rocking chair, propped my foot up on the bed, and felt thoroughly sorry for myself. I had gone up and down mountain trails, I had climbed over boulders, I had waded through snow, mud and slush, with no damage to myself whatever. Then, on my own doorstep . . . Vicki laid her head in my lap and whined her sympathy. This brought me out of my doldrums. I gently scratched her ears.

"Never mind, Vicki," I said. "Remember, I have young legs, so I'll get over this in a jiffy."

Brave words, but things didn't work out that way. In a few hours I could scarcely hobble around the cabin. When the boys came down from the mine and found out what had happened, they were deeply concerned.

"I'll lay off work tomorrow and take you to the doctor at Yreka," Dearsir stated firmly.

"Thanks a lot," I said. "But that won't be necessary. It's probably nothing more than a strained muscle. My ankle isn't even swollen. See?" I stretched them both out for comparison.

"Hm-m-m, that's right, it isn't," agreed Up'nUp. "You've got real nice ankles, Dear Mad'm. But just the same, there's one of 'em you can't walk on very good. Better let one of us take you to Yreka."

"Couldn't think of it," I said airily. "You boys are working hard at the mine now. One of you gone, and the other wouldn't get much gravel washed. Takes two on that job; one on the end of a shovel, the other to hold the Little Giant. A few days from now this leg will be as good as new."

Reluctantly they finally gave in.

But I continued to limp and there was more pain that I let the boys know about. Dearsir brought me a stout oaken cane that he had made from a fairly straight branch, with a knob whittled smooth to fit my hand. I used it to get around the cabin and yard and it did help, but I hated it. The thought of becoming a cane addict filled me with gloom. Somehow, a cane suggests a feeble old age that is going to get worse as time passes. Now I may be old, I thought, but I am not feeble —so being forced to use a cane was a real cross.

Was this going to be permanent? I asked myself as day after day went by, with my leg showing no improvement. If so, I would have to give up my adventure of living in the Klamath Forest. I couldn't see myself as a quitter, and had no notion of letting this happen. But what was I to do? The question followed me around all day and would not let me sleep nights. A week, then ten days, went by. Something had to be done. But what? I was determined not to ask the boys to stop work on their claims and take me to a doctor at Yreka.

Finally I had an inspiration. The solution of the problem was so simple that I berated myself for not having thought of it before. I would go with Tom in the mail truck to the hospital on the Indian Reservation at Hoopa, see the doctor there, then come home with Tom on his return trip the same day. When the boys stopped in on their way from work that evening, I told them my plan. They agreed that it was a good one.

Next morning I hobbled down to the mail box a few minutes before seven o'clock, bundled up in a warm sweater under my woolliest coat, and carrying my cane. I really needed it to get down my trail to the road. Right on time, Tom's light truck rounded the curve. I hailed him and he stopped.

"How come?" he asked, looking at my cane as he helped me into the seat.

"It's an ornament I'm wearing to Hoopa."

"Ornament, nothing! You're not old enough for a cane."

No wonder I like Tom.

When we arrived at Hoopa Tom drove me to the hospital and helped me out. "You can pick me up at the post office on your way back this afternoon," I said. Tom nodded and drove away. I went up the path and into the doctor's office. He was an anemic elderly gentleman who gazed at me through huge black-bowed bifocals and diagnosed my case coldly and brutally.

Old age, he said.

He didn't ask me any questions about occupation, previous illnesses, or present symptoms. He didn't feel my pulse, take my temperature, or even look at my teeth. I am sure he saw me through the window of his office as I limped up the walk; a small, stooped, overweight, white-haired woman—a wholly uninteresting figure. He had me placed before I entered the door of the hospital; had mentally tabulated everything from the number of the mimeographed diet sheet to the prescription he intended to give me.

He handed me what appeared to be a diet sheet—I haven't read it yet—and a prescription—I haven't had it filled yet —for some kind of vitamins. He outlined a program for every hour of the twenty-four—twelve hours in bed, sleeping; two hours in the morning and two in the afternoon resting in a relaxed position; two fifteen-minute periods of mild exercise . . .

I interrupted him, called his attention to my two young legs, one in perfect condition, the other slightly damaged.

He wasn't listening. Or even looking.

"A cane," he said. "You will find it useful."

"I already have a cane, doctor, and I don't like canes. Perhaps a crutch—a new one, please—all bright and shiny—"

Resignedly, he rose and brought me one. I paid him and walked out, leaving the oak cane leaning against my chair. The crutch worked very well. Nothing had been done for my leg, but I felt pleased with myself, anyway. A crutch, especially a new, cheap one, suggests a merely temporary ailment, like a sprained ankle or a broken leg. It intimates that some day soon you'll set the crutch behind a door and walk out bravely and steadily, forgetting all about it. Not at all like a cane.

I had lunch at the little restaurant where I had eaten the day I was on my way to the cabin. The pretty Hoopa waitress remembered me, greeted me cheerfully. It was all very warm and friendly. She asked me to wait there where I could be comfortable until Tom came.

In the course of time he drove up to the post office and a little later came walking into the restaurant.

"Thought I'd find you here," he said. "It's cold today, even in the sun. Glad to see you've got a crutch. Lots better than a cane. What'd the doctor say?"

"Very little," I said truthfully. "So I guess there's nothing much the matter with me."

He nodded, told the waitress what he wanted for lunch, ate it, and we rose to go. I followed him to the mail truck and he settled me and my crutch in the cab. And off we went, following the clear and lovely Trinity River until it flowed into the Klamath at Weitchpec. After that the road wound along by the rolling jade waters of the Klamath. I like to ride with Tom. I talk and talk. He listens and listens. Discreet, noncommittal, knows everything about everybody—and never tells what he shouldn't.

We rode along in the rapidly chilling afternoon until we came to Orleans, a bright, clean little village set among green pines and fir trees, surrounded by towering mountains. There we picked up another passenger. I caught only a glimpse of him as two men half-carried, half-dragged him off the store porch, heaved him into the open bed of the truck, and jammed an old felt hat down on his head. Then they put a glass gallon jug and a flour sack apparently filled with an assortment of groceries in beside him.

When Tom had driven away I asked him about the passenger.

"Don't you think he must be terribly uncomfortable back there?"

"Oh, he doesn't mind. That's where he always rides."

"But he's sick—"

"He's an old drunk, and I'm getting mighty tired of hauling him back to his cabin. And for nothing. He never remembers to pay me."

I was horrified.

"Do you mean to say this happens all the time?"

"Every month, regular as clockwork. He comes down to Orleans, cashes his pension check, gets a few groceries and a gallon of wine. Then he sits in the saloon drinking beer until he's dead drunk. The barkeep has to drag him out and get somebody to help load him onto me to deliver. I'm getting plenty tired of it."

"Where does he live, Tom?"

"Up here a ways—a few miles this side of Somesbar. I'll put him off at the side of the road and leave him there. When he sobers up enough, he can make his way down to his cabin."

As we rolled along over the next few miles I thought scornfully now and then of the old sot in the back of the truck. After a while Tom drew up at the side of the road, went around to the back, dragged the drunk man out and carried him over to a pine tree. Coming back, he got the jug and flour sack, put them down by the man's side. Tom stood looking at the old fellow for a moment, as if uncertain what to do next. Then, leaning down, he dragged the unconscious man to a sitting position, braced his back against a tree.

The old man's head lolled to one side and his battered hat fell off. I got my first full view of his face. The skin was like white parchment stretched over bones, eyes wide open but unseeing like the eyes of a blind man. From his loose, shabby coat sleeves two small bony hands protruded; the hands of a man who had never done hard labor—frail, delicate and appealing. My heart filled with pity for this human derelict.

The sun was behind the mountain now, the air felt definitely colder. Tom got in the car, but he didn't touch the starter. I looked at him enquiringly.

"I'm thinking what if a bear or a cougar comes across the old coot tonight," he said. "I shouldn't leave him like this, but I can't very well take him with me."

"Didn't you say he had a cabin around here?"

"Yes. Down there in the brush somewhere. It's too far for me to carry him. And there isn't much more than a cow trail for a road. It would be dangerous to drive the truck down it."

"Let me take a look." I grabbed my crutch, climbed out and went over to the brink of the slope that ended at the River several hundred feet below.

"The road's not too bad. I believe you can make it," I called.

Tom took my word for it. He crawled out of the cab, picked the old man up, got him back in the truck, then put the jug and sack of groceries in beside him. He carefully edged the truck onto the steep, deeply rutted road, while I watched anxiously. The rough jolting partially roused the old man. He pulled himself to his knees by clutching the tailgate with his fragile, bony fingers and tried to clamber out.

I hurriedly limped after the slowly moving truck and slapped his hands smartly with my leather gloves. He let go and dropped back into the bed of the truck. Again he pulled himself up and again I slapped his hands until he let go and fell back. We kept this up all the while Tom bumped and lurched over rock and rain-washed gashes in the roadway. I must have hurt the old man's hands, but it seemed I had to do it.

All the time his eyes looked at me with an expression of abject terror. No mere woman could possibly be doing this to him. Probably, in his drunken fancy I was an evil witch, a bloodsucking vampire, pursuing him with intent to do him even greater harm.

When Tom stopped before a tumbledown cabin and came around the truck to help him, the old man threw his arms around Tom's neck and began to sob like a child. Tom picked him up gently, trying to sooth his hysterical fright, and carried him into the stoutly fenced yard, as I held the wire gate open. A faithful dog waited on the porch. He seemed to understand his master's condition, making no protest when Tom laid the old man down and covered him with several sacks that evidently were the dog's bed. He immediately sank once more into a stupor.

Tom began to search for a key so that he could take the old fellow inside. He looked under the step, over the window, kicked a box aside. No key. He started to go through the man's pants-pockets, but at the first touch, bony fingers grasped Tom's in a viselike grip.

"Some heel must have robbed him." Tom stood thinking for a moment.

"There's nothing more I can do," he said finally, "but leave him here on the porch with his dog to guard him. The fence will protect him from wild animals." Tom put his jug and groceries beside the sleeping figure.

We climbed into the truck and drove back up the steep, rough trail to the road. Tom spoke wonderingly of the terror he had seen in the old man's eyes when he lifted him out of the truck. I explained the tactics I had used to keep him from jumping out.

"He's not used to women," Tom said. "You may have scared him so he'll stay sober after this."

"I have no such hope. Tom, it's going to get awfully cold on that porch before morning."

"Yeah." His face set in a worried frown.

Twenty-one

TOM let me out at the foot of my trail and went on to Happy Camp, the end of his route. By the time Vicki and I had eaten our suppers, the darkness of the winter night closed in. All the hobbling around I had done that day on my sore leg hadn't done it any good. It pained me severely. Feeling slightly desperate, I did what I should have done in the first place; put hot compresses on it every five minutes for an hour. The pain lessened to a faint ache and I went to bed.

But not to sleep. I kept seeing that poor emaciated figure lying on the cabin porch far down the canyon, the dog crouched close by. It turned very cold, so cold that I crept out of bed, got another blanket from the closet and spread it on top of my others. While I was up I looked at the thermometer. The mercury was six degrees below freezing. I climbed into bed, shivering under my warm blankets.

Around two o'clock I heard the metallic clickity-click of an ancient car being driven swiftly by, headed down the road. I wondered how anyone dared drive at such breakneck speed in the dark and around the sharp turns. Time passed. The thought of the old man gave me no peace. He would be dead by morning, the poor dog helpless to revive him.

At half past four the same car I had heard go by before, came rushing up the River; I recognized it by the sharp clickity-click it made. Who would be driving furiously up and down the road in the night? At five o'clock it was still pitch-dark, but I got up, lit my lamp and made a fire on the cookstove. Soon the cabin was cozily warm, filled with the good smell of coffee and sizzling bacon.

When it drew near to seven o'clock I bundled myself up, and with the help of my crutch—though my leg felt better this morning—hobbled down to the mailbox where I planned to stop Tom and talk to him.

"Hello," Tom said, coming to a stop, right on time as usual. "Here's two letters and the *Siskiyou News*. What are you doing down here this time of the morning? You should have waited for the boys to bring the mail up to you."

"Tom, I had to see you. I worried all night about that poor old man."

"I didn't. Not all night, anyway. Only till twelve o'clock. Then I jumped out of bed, got into my coupe and drove like hell down the River to his cabin. I broke in the door—don't know why I didn't do it in the first place; just naturally too law-abiding, I guess. I dragged the old soak inside, started to undress him—found the key in his shirt pocket. Never thought of looking there. Got him into bed, then made him drink two cups of scalding hot coffee to warm him up. When I left him he was sleeping. Then I drove like hell back to Happy Camp so as to get there in time to pick up the morning mail from Yreka. Made it, too."

Tears filled my eyes.

"I—I heard you, Tom. You drove more than seventy-five miles over a dangerous road to save the life of a disreputable old soak. He should be eternally grateful to you."

"Not he," Tom said with a short laugh. "He'll wake up nice and warm in his bed this morning and think he had a bad dream about a wicked old witch who slapped his hands. Oh, well, there's a lot more to carrying the mail on a Star Route than delivering letters and looking after parcel-post packages."

He jammed his foot on the starter and drove down the road like a madman.

I took my time getting back to the cabin. That pesky leg. The pain wasn't so bad as it had been the night before, but definitely worse than before my visit to the doctor at Hoopa. Not that I blamed him, I thought, trying to be just. If I were foolish enough to hobble down a practically impassable mountain road in an effort to save an old drunk from the consequences of his folly, I deserved to have an aching leg. I was repeating the hot compress treatment when the boys stopped in to get a report on my trip. I told them about it. They both looked serious.

"What about going to Yreka tomorrow?" Dearsir asked anxiously. "I'd be glad to—"

"Nothing doing. I'm planning to treat this leg myself for a few days, at the same time keeping off it as much as possible. I'll be fine—you'll see." This was plain whistling in the dark, but the boys didn't know that. I was haunted by the fear that this might mean I would be forced to leave the lovely Klamath country I had come to love, live out the rest of my days carefully, my life limited by a crutch.

The boys went on up to the mine and I settled down grimly to staying inside for a few days. It was just as well, because I had to stay there anyway. By noon the sky was overcast with dark gray clouds and when morning came at least a foot of snow lay on the ground, with more fluttering down softly and continuously. The limbs of the trees drooped under their chilly burden and everywhere there was a white stillness.

I propped my foot up on a chair and at intervals of an hour

or so, wrapped my leg in hot towels. My recovery was dramatically rapid. By the end of the week, when the storm cleared away, I put the crutch behind a door and forgot it, just as I had hoped I could. All along the River the snow melted rapidly. While the snow covered the ground around my cabin, I had missed my beautiful little friends, the mountain quail, who had been coming down to visit me. Now I began to watch for their return. But day after day passed with no sign of them, no sound of their soft calls. Perhaps they had been frightened away—or perhaps they were starving up there on the mountain where snow must still be lying, cold and deep.

So one morning when I was quite well again, I belted on my slicker, donned a new pair of boots Dearsir had bought for me in Happy Camp, stuffed a small canvas bag with crushed barley and set out on my jaunt in search of the quail. Soon I was beyond the mud and slush and into snow that became deeper and deeper as I went up the mountainside. Still no sight or sound of quail. Perhaps if I called them . . .

What was their call like, anyway? I couldn't remember clearly. I tried a low whistle. It sounded pretty good. I whistled louder. Still louder . . . and heard a faint echo from across the canyon. Then there came another sound— a sort of mixture of laughing hyena, excited blue jay, and a hysterical human being. This frightened me to a standstill. Then something came bearing down on me through the trees—my old enemy, Pete!

He approached me with a strangely uneven, humping gait, his mouth wide open, tail sticking straight out behind, braying at every step. I leaped behind the nearest tree. Fortunately, it had a trunk at least four feet thick. An instant later Pete was on the other side. His ears came in sight around one side, pointing forward. I darted to the other side, only to find Pete there ahead of me. We kept this up for what

seemed a long time, but it probably wasn't over fifteen
seconds. Then I had an inspiration. When Pete and I faced

each other again, I threw the sack of barley and hit him on
the nose.

That did it.

Pete stayed where he was, got his nose inside the bag and began to munch barley industriously. I ran as fast as my young legs would carry me down the trail to the cabin. When I recovered my breath and realized I was safe, I remembered Pete's lumbering gait after me—and more especially, I realized now, after my barley. It came to me clearly—Pete was using only three legs. That was why he humped along as he had. He was lame.

Poor old Pete. I must talk to Dearsir about it the first time the boys stopped in. As much as I wanted to help the quail, I couldn't go up on that trail again carrying barley, that grain evidently being Pete's idea of a magnificent treat.

Dearsir stopped in early next morning. Over a cup of coffee he told me that Up'nUp had taken the jalopy and left for Yreka to see Nora and little Benji. He'd be gone several days. There were plenty of one-man jobs at the mine now, piling gravel and such, so he couldn't chat long.

"I saw Pete yesterday," I said, leaving out how far up the mountain I had gone, the sack of barley, and Pete's pursuit of me—or of the barley.

"I haven't seen the old fellow for quite a spell. Where was he?"

"Oh, up the trail a little way," I said vaguely. "He's very lame."

"Confound it! That's probably my fault. I forgot about his hoofs. They should have been trimmed weeks ago. We're going to need him in the next few days to drag lumber up to the mine from the road. Up'nUp will bring some back when he comes. But I can't take care of Pete without help."

"What has to be done?"

"I told you, Dear Mad'm, Pete's hoofs have to be trimmed. They're probably an inch longer by now than they should be. No wonder the poor old boy has to hobble along."

"My goodness! How does anyone trim a mule's hoofs?"

"With a chisel and rasp," he said absently.

"Poor Pete! How it must hurt him."

"No, no." Dearsir was a little impatient at my ignorance. "It won't hurt Pete at all, any more than trimming your fingernails hurts you. But I have to have that mule in shape to work when Up'nUp gets back from Yreka and he'll need a few days after the job's done to get used to walking on his trimmed hoofs. I wonder if Frenchy—no, too much temper. You never know what he'll do—likely he'd get mad at Pete, draw off and kick him. I can't take any chances on having Pete mistreated, or even frightened."

I thought guiltily of the time I had hit Pete with a rock —and directed a stream of water in his ear.

"I know!" Dearsir exclaimed. "You can help me. All you have to do is hold his halter rope."

"Oh, no, Dearsir," I said, shrinking back. "Please—I don't think Pete likes me very well—"

"Don't be unreasonable. Why should Pete dislike you? He's the friendliest mule I ever knew." He pushed back his coffee cup and rose. "I'll go right now and find him. It won't take me long. He always comes when I whistle for him. We'll come back by Bent Pine and get the tools I'll need. You can look for us in about an hour. This can't be put off." And he was gone up the trail, whistling something that sounded remarkably like my call to the quail.

I was left alone with my misgivings, and they were serious ones. If Pete was a friendly mule, I devoutly hoped I'd never meet an unfriendly one. However, I had to admit that my approach to him when we first met had not been one to arouse in him a feeling of warm regard toward me. Perhaps if I were a little more tactful . . . but how does one go about being tactful to a mule? I was thoroughly frightened at the prospect of assisting in giving Pete a manicure—no, a pedicure, I corrected myself miserably.

In less than an hour Dearsir led Pete up the trail from the road and into my back yard. I timidly opened the door.

"Dear Mad'm, if you'll step out here and hold this halter, I'll begin operations," was Dearsir's casual approach to what seemed to me a very serious situation indeed.

I walked toward Pete warily, clutched the halter rope with deep misgivings. Pete turned his head and looked at me; balefully, I thought, then turned his gaze up the mountainside as if I were beneath his notice. I took heart. All I asked was that he pay no attention whatever to me.

Dearsir picked up Pete's right front foot, held it between his knees and examined it critically. "Just as I expected," he declared. "Hoof's a good inch longer than it ought to be. I'll see what I can do with the rasp first. Gol darn it, I oughtn't to have neglected him this way. Good old Pete—"

The big brute turned his head, jerked his foot away, nearly upsetting Dearsir.

"Hang onto the halter, woman!" snapped Dearsir. "Here, up close to the head—like this."

I obeyed, venturing a little pat on Pete's neck and a hopefully hypocritical, "There, there! Good old Pete——" broken off abruptly as he again turned his head and looked me up and down with—did I imagine it?—less contemptuous animosity than before. Could it be?

By this time Dearsir had retrieved a block of wood from the woodshed. "I can see the rasp's too slow for this job," he said, "except putting on the finishing touches. I'll have to use the chisel."

By dint of much hammering, much careful placing of the sharp chisel, followed by judicious use of the rasp, Pete's right front hoof was finally pared down and shaped to Dearsir's satisfaction. But Pete had been so restless that both Dearsir and I were worn out.

"Got to do something to keep him still," Dearsir said. "Tell you what, I'll get your sack of bird feed and set it under his nose. That ought to do the trick."

He got an almost empty gunny sack from the cellar. Pete sniffed excitedly, buried his nose in the crushed barley and began a steady champing. Wonderful. This was all that was needed to quiet his nerves. Our troubles were over. I sighed with relief.

There was no more difficulty—until Dearsir began to work on the fourth hoof, which happened to be a hind one. Suddenly Pete began to twitch in sundry places, tried to pull his leg out of Dearsir's grasp. I had been watching Dearsir. Now I turned to Pete in consternation to see what was causing his actions.

The last grain of barley was gone.

"Hang on to him!" Dearsir shouted. "I gotta finish this hoof! Feed him more barley!"

"Where'll I get it, I'd like to know?" I expected no answer. The situation was strictly up to me. Certainly Dearsir, at Pete's rear and hanging onto the mule's hoof for dear life, was in no position to do anything. Remembering my hint of success when using similar guileful tactics a short time before, I spoke honeyed words in Pete's ear. I patted his neck. I recklessly promised him unlimited barley—as soon as I could get it. I don't know what all I said, to the accompaniment of the quick rasp-rasp-rasp of the giant file against that hind hoof.

At last Dearsir eased Pete's foot to the ground, wiped his face with his handkerchief.

"There," he said with satisfaction. "Now you see, it wasn't much of a job, after all. Thanks to you for helping me, Dear Mad'm."

"You're welcome." I handed him Pete's halter rope, glad that my skirt hid the trembling of my knees. "I think I'll lie down for a while." I started toward the back door.

"Good idea," he said. "But you wouldn't go without saying goodbye to Pete, would you?"

I turned. "Oh, not for worlds!" Staggering slightly, I walked back until I stood at Pete's head. I knew how to handle him. Fearlessly I reached up and scratched his head at the base of those enormous ears. He turned a little, gently pressed his surprisingly velvety nose against my shoulder.

"Goodbye, Pete," I said.

"You see?" Dearsir volunteered triumphantly. "I told you he is the friendliest mule in the whole Klamath Forest. Now do you believe me?"

"Yes, I believe you." I gave Pete's head a parting scratch. "But just the same, I'm going to lie down a little while."

Twenty-two

———◆•••▶———

TWO weeks went by, with life going on in a pleasantly monotonous way for Vicki and me. There was quite a bit of rain, which pleased the boys, even though it meant they had to work in rubber boots and slickers most of the time. The rain assured them of a good supply of water in the flumes they had built during the months they could not wash gravel. They had started washing gravel about the first of December, that being the date when the legal ban against this phase of placer mining was lifted. Now they worked every hour they could, hoping to have a good cleanup on the first of February. The rain brought the sound of the River from a murmur to a low, continuous roar.

Then for a day and a night snow fell, thick and soft, turning our world to one in which no green showed, everything being different shades of white. The *Siskiyou News* said that the snowfall was much heavier on the upper reaches of the River in Oregon than it was in our part of the country. I thought that was good, since it meant more water would sink into the ground to replenish springs as the snow slowly melted, but the boys did not share my optimistic outlook. They just shook their heads without bothering to explain, and hurried off to the mine, regardless of the snow that covered the ground.

A few days later I woke one morning and sensed at once that the River had a deeper note than before. Mixed with that I heard another sound—gentle rain on the roof a few feet above my head. That meant the weather had turned warmer and I was glad. I never did like severe cold. The rain would soon melt the snow and my mountain world would be green again.

A little while later the boys came into my kitchen, their slickers dripping.

"Here's your mail," Dearsir said, pulling the *Siskiyou News* and two circulars from an inside pocket. "There's some news in the paper that might interest you."

I spread it on the table. A big black headline stared up at me.

FLOOD WARNING

Quickly I read the paragraph below. It stated that two unprecedentedly heavy cloudbursts had occurred the day before on the upper Klamath. This deluge of rain had melted millions of tons of snow. The result was an alarming rise in the River. The crest of the flood had not yet reached Siskiyou County, and its height could not be forecast at the present time.

I looked at the boys. Their faces were grave.

"What—what will happen?" I asked.

"There's no telling," Dearsir said. "The River is three feet higher this morning than it was last night. Bent Pine—well, you know those four crooked pine trees. Their trunks are bent about four feet above the ground—maybe ten feet higher than the River is now. That'll give you an idea. If the River rose that much once it can do it again."

"If it does, it will sweep away the cabin—"

"Yep," Up'nUp said. "But Dear Mad'm, the River's nowhere near that high now. We ain't going to worry until we have to—"

"Up'nUp's right," Dearsir broke in. "He and I are going on up to the mine now, but we'll be down about noon to see how things are. Now, don't you worry. Probably nothing at all will happen. And you're safe, regardless of what kind of tantrum the River has. Your cabin is at least a hundred feet above the highest water mark the old Klamath ever left."

They strode off through the rain, which had lessened to a mere drizzle, leaving me restless, oppressed with dread of what might happen at Bent Pine. How could those boys have gone off up the mountainside? Pete and the nannies—they were free and had sense enough to take care of themselves. But those fool chickens—of course, their fenced yard was well back from the River, but closer to it than the cabin . . . but, I reminded myself, there was nothing I could do. They would go berserk with fear if I so much as approached them. And the boys surely knew what they were doing—they'd lived for years in this country.

The rain stopped, the skies cleared to a beautiful blue. From my first terrace I could look down on the tossing, muddy River, hear it roar as it surged by, angry and threatening, overwhelming in its power. Shivering, I went inside and waited for the boys to come back. At eleven I put on my high rubber boots, laid my woolly coat and yellow slicker on the bed. I was going to Bent Pine with them, and nothing they could say was going to stop me.

When they did come we had quite an argument, but in the end I went along. When we reached Bent Pine, we walked down the roadway and past the tool house before we could see how high the River had risen. Dirty water swirled where the garden had been, its frothy waves gnawing at the foot of the first of the four crooked pine trees. Part of the chicken yard was under water, the hens huddled in the mud next to their house, cluck-clucking in mad terror. The little orchard had not as yet been touched by the rising flood, and the cabin and tool house looked safe—at least for a time.

Dearsir found a four-foot-long stick and pushed it into the ground at the edge of the water, then cut a notch at the water level with his pocket knife.

"We'll use that as a gauge," he said, "to tell whether the water is rising or falling. Let's go into the cabin, get warm, and have something to eat. The chickens are in no danger for a while."

Up'nUp heated beans, made coffee; Dearsir set the table. We ate in silence—except for the ominous roar of the River, so close to us. It was a dreadful sound and I was unable to get the sight of the wild tossing flood out of my mind. Finally we rose from the table and went to look at Dearsir's improvised gauge. The notch was hidden by brown water. Dearsir pulled up the stick, looked at it carefully.

"There's been a four-inch rise while we were eating," he said. "We better take care of those chickens, Up'nUp."

He set up the gauge again. Then the boys caught the bedraggled and terrified hens by their feet and carried them six at a time to the goats' barn across the road and a little way up the mountainside, shutting them inside. The poor squawking things. With so little brain it is hard to know how they could become so frightened.

We went back into the cabin and waited. At intervals one or the other of the boys went out and examined the gauge. Hour by hour the water rose until the ground where the fruit trees grew was covered to the depth of six inches. So strong was the current of the River that even this shallow water swirled and frothed, advancing and retreating, leaving edges of yellow foam that were carried away by the next surge. It was as if the River reached out in ravening anger, obsessed by the passion to destroy everything it could reach.

We were too oppressed by the sense of danger to read, so we talked idly of this and that, trying to forget the threat of the River.

"There was a man, a stranger, name of Bill Shaw, at Happy Camp the last time I was there," Dearsir said. "Got to talking to him. He and his partner have located a placer claim on the other side of the River about a mile below Fuchsia Point."

"Across the River!" exploded Up'nUp. "Now there's a bright pair! How they going to get stuff across? You can't do much with a boat, even when it's safe to use one—which isn't often."

"They aim to build a suspension bridge, like the one the Bennings have."

"That'll cost 'em some money," Up'nUp observed.

"Sure it will," said Dearsir, "but from the way Shaw talked, they didn't mind that. He thinks they have a rich claim over there. What started me thinking about him—this flood will delay them for a while. They aren't going to like that. There's only about five months left for them to wash gravel before summer comes, and it will take them a while to get set up for it."

"How'd he plan to get the first cable across the River?" I asked.

"He has a power boat he intends to use, he told me. But now it isn't going to be safe to do that for a while. Sometimes it takes the old River quite a spell to settle down after one of these rampages."

"I'm glad it's him and not me that's going to work across the River," Up'nUp said. "The whole idea is crazy, if you ask me. I hope he ain't going to ask us to help him get that cable across."

Dearsir looked uncomfortable. "Probably he will," he said.

"I think he kind of got the impression that I said we would—I don't know how—"

Up'nUp gave Dearsir a disgusted look. "Knowin' you, I bet I know how he got that impression. You gave it to him. You're the original fall guy for every feller in the Siskiyous that tells you he needs help. Oh, well, I guess it won't hurt us to lend him and his partner a hand."

"It'll likely be some time in the future," Dearsir said, and got up to go look at his gauge again. I went with him, stood at the edge of the water, now only a few feet from the cabin, feeling the power of the River in my very bones. The Klamath, even in summer, is never a peaceful, pretty stream, as are so many of the small rivers and creeks flowing into it. Always it is a river of rugged, austere beauty, traveling tumultuously toward the sea. In flood, as it was now, its power overshadowed every other characteristic, and I looked at it appalled. It could so easily sweep away the home of my two friends, as if it were no more than a frail matchbox.

But we were spared that calamity. At four o'clock the flood reached its crest, paused there a while, and then began to subside. By dark it had gone down a foot, and we went into the cabin for supper. That over, the boys took me home.

"But won't you be afraid to go to sleep?" I asked them as we said goodnight. "The water might rise again."

"I'll keep watch until midnight," Dearsir answered. "Then Up'nUp can take over. But I hardly think there is any danger."

I went to bed and quickly fell asleep, in spite of the roaring of the River in the canyon below me.

The River went down almost as fast as it had risen, but not to its old level. The water stayed high and rough, the current swift and treacherous.

One morning the boys stopped by to tell me they were on

their way down the River to help Jim Shaw and his partner get their first cable across the River in preparation for building the suspension footbridge.

"I don't think we'll be gone long, though," Dearsir said. "In my opinion, it isn't safe to take a boat out on the River yet—not even a powerful one such as Jim Shaw's—though the water at that point flows more smoothly than most places. The swirling currents are completely unpredictable and highly dangerous."

"We told Jim we'd be down, so we gotta go," Up'nUp said. "But it's a wild-goose chase. We knew you'd hear the jalopy go by, so we thought we better tell you where we were headed for."

"Thank you, boys," I said. "Now you be sure you don't let this Jim Shaw persuade you to do anything foolish."

"Haw!" was Up'nUp's comment. "Don't you worry, Dear Mad'm. We're not going to risk our necks out in no boat, with the Klamath kicking up like it is. We're just going to help Jim and his partner get the cable out of the truck and fixed so as it'll unwind off the reel without no hitch. Him and his partner aim to handle the boat."

"The cable is heavy," Dearsir said. "I'm not sure we can lift the reel out of the truck and get it down to the edge of the River. We'll stop and get Frenchy to go along. He can lift more than any other three men I know."

"Maybe he won't go," I ventured, not liking any part of this.

"Of course he will," Dearsir answered a little impatiently. "Frenchy's always glad to lend a hand to anybody. And you know how proud he is of his strength. He's like a kid, wanting to show it off. Well, we better be on our way."

"Please stop on your way back," I said. "I want to know how you make out."

"Sure will, Dear Mad'm," Up'nUp promised.

A few minutes afterward their jalopy went chugging off down the road.

It was almost two hours later when I heard the boys' footsteps coming up my trail. I hurried to the door, threw it open.

"Hello!" I called. "How did—" The sight of their faces stopped me. I knew something dreadful had happened. But what? They were both here, apparently safe and sound. Wordlessly they came in and sat down. I sank into my wicker rocking chair, knees weak with dread.

"What is it?" I asked. Up'nUp looked appealingly at Dearsir.

"Frenchy's dead," Dearsir said.

"No! How—what—" My mouth felt dry and I clutched the arms of my chair, leaning forward.

"Drowned," he said. "I can't believe it myself yet. But I saw him . . ."

He stopped as if unable to continue.

"Up'nUp, tell me."

But Up'nUp, his face buried in his hands, was beyond speech.

"It was like this," Dearsir began with an effort. "We all agreed, after one look at the River, that it would be suicide to try crossing in the boat. Jim and his partner were very much upset by the delay in their plans. Delay was serious, of course. They haven't much time to work their claims before the first of July. However, they gave up the whole idea of getting the cable across until the River went down more.

"Then Frenchy spoke up. He ordered us to tie one end of a carpenter's chalk line to the cable. He would, he declared, take the other end of the chalk line in his hand, swim with it to the opposite bank of the River, haul the cable across and fasten it to a big fir tree there. That would solve the problem. He was absolutely sure he could do it."

"And you men *let* him?" I cried.

"We couldn't stop him. You know how Frenchy is. The more we opposed him, the more stubborn he acted. He got the idea we thought he wasn't strong enough to do it— which was of course the truth—and he made up his mind he'd show us. Why, we even refused to tie the chalk line to the cable. So he did it himself.

"Then he took off his shoes, grabbed the cord, and walked into the water. Ten feet from the bank, the current grabbed him—swept him downstream fast. But he kept making some headway toward the opposite shore. About two-thirds of the way across, the River swirled around a big rock. Between it and the farther bank the water, though racing along, was comparatively smooth. Frenchy reached this rock, pulled himself out of the water, stood up. He grinned at us, raised the fist with the cord grasped in it, and waved. He yelled something, we couldn't hear what. Then, suddenly, he pitched backwards. The lashing, boiling currents around the rock sucked him under in an instant. We never saw him again."

"But—but—what do you suppose happened?"

"Dear Mad'm, we'll never know. His foot may have slipped on the rock—his heart may have failed because of the terrific exertion of battling the currents of the River."

"But wouldn't an autopsy—"

"We hunted for miles down the River," Up'nUp said. "No sight of him."

"The body of anyone who drowns in the Klamath is almost never found," Dearsir said. "With water as high as it is now, I think there is no chance we will ever see Frenchy again."

Dearsir was right. The River had claimed him forever.

Though Frenchy had kept himself apart and aloof from everyone, he had always been kind and generous. The folks up and down the Klamath missed him; missed the sight of his great figure striding by on the road, the sound of his booming laughter. His cabin, which could be seen clearly from the road, soon looked untenanted, the railing of the tiny ramshackle bridge he used to cross a little stream broke and no one repaired it. This weatherbeaten cabin and the flimsy, dilapidated bridge constituted the only monument Frenchy had to remind people that he had ever lived.

Twenty-three

———◆◆◆◆▶———

NEXT to the last day in January the boys decided to clean the gold dust and nuggets out of the riffles in their sluice boxes, find out what their reward was to be for their strenuous two months' work since the last cleanup. From their talk I discovered that what I had thought to be a barbecue grill the day I cleaned up the tool house was really a small forge which they used with a good-sized retort to recover gold from the quicksilver.

I should have liked to go up to Bent Pine and watch the last stages of their cleanup, but they disregarded my hints for an invitation. I couldn't say I blamed them. They had a job to do—one that was important to them—and they didn't want to be distracted from their work by questions and comments from a rank amateur in the business of placer mining. But they knew how interested I was in the outcome, so after they finished weighing the gold, they came down to my cabin to report.

"Not too good, and not too bad," was Dearsir's judicial summing-up of the situation. "We'll realize about two thousand dollars on the deal. And there are about five more months to wash gravel before the state shuts down on us for the summer. But we'll clean up again about the first of April."

"What are you going to do with the gold, boys?"

Dearsir answered me. "We decided to take it to Happy Camp first thing in the morning, send it by express from there to the mint in San Francisco. Do you want us to do some shopping for you?"

"Well, what I'd really like is to go with you. That is, if you're going early enough. I've been hoping for a long time I'd get a chance to go to Yreka for a day and visit Nora and Benji. I can get a bus out of Happy Camp about nine o'clock."

"Sure, that'll be swell," Up'nUp said. "Then we'll come back and pick you up about five or six in the afternoon."

"Well, that's settled," Dearsir said, rising to go. "What's left of the day, Up'nUp and I will work on the trail up to the mine. It's almost finished now. By the time good weather comes, you'll be able to go up there any time you want to."

"Thanks a lot. That will be fine."

"We'll stop by for you about seven in the morning," Dearsir said, and they went whistling down the trail.

I had another reason for wanting to go to Yreka. But I hadn't mentioned it to the boys for fear they would laugh at me. I intended to go to a doctor there for a checkup. Not that there was anything special the matter with me, but I'd read a very convincing, even scary, article in a magazine saying that everyone should have a medical going-over every six months regardless of how well he felt. I decided to do it the first chance I got, and this was it.

Next morning everything went according to schedule, and at ten minutes after nine the boys waved goodbye to me as I boarded a bus at Happy Camp and set off for my visit with Nora and that checkup with a doctor. Arriving at my destination, a taxi took me to Up'nUp's little white house on the outskirts of town. Here Nora greeted me with exuberant joy.

"Come in, Dear Mad'm!" she called, standing in the doorway. Then she ran down the path to meet me, lifted me off my feet in her strong young arms, set me down carefully as if I were breakable.

We went inside and she showed me little Benji—though he wasn't very little any more. He lay in his crib, plump, rosy and beautiful, talking to himself.

"Kinda nice, isn't he?" she said, the glow of pride in her voice more than offsetting the understatement of her words.

"He's wonderful, Nora." And I meant it. She beamed at me.

Somewhat to my surprise, Benji was immaculate, the house clean and orderly. What was more, I knew Nora kept it that way. No woman can fool another woman about a thing like that. When it came to fundamentals, Nora was all right, whether in matters of love, or of housekeeping.

She served us a delicious luncheon of creamed chicken, hot biscuit, lettuce-and-tomato salad, with vanilla ice cream for dessert. She knew I didn't often get ice cream down on the Klamath. We ate slowly, lingered over our coffee afterward, talking of many things, mostly the baby. Finally we got around to the baby's father.

"Nora," I said cautiously, "what about Up'nUp? Do you think he'll ever get a town job and live here with you and Benji?"

"Why, yes, Dear Mad'm," she said seriously. "I'm expecting he will. Right now, I'm giving him plenty of slack. He hasn't really grown up yet, some ways."

"I know. But some men never get over loving the freedom of the mountains, the joy of working for themselves, and the gamble, the excitement of mining. Maybe he—"

"Oh, I'm sure he will," she replied. "He's all right. I love him, and I'm dead certain he loves me—and the baby, too. Benji and I can wait. When he's ready, he'll come to us. And I don't want him any sooner."

"We-e-ell, I hope you're right," I said doubtfully. "But Nora, he's so happy there at the claims—he loves the mountains and the river. Transplant him into town and—well, I don't know . . ." I paused, then took the plunge.

"Nora, dear, did you ever think that you and Benji might come to Bent Pine to live?"

Her eyes grew round with astonishment.

"No, Dear Mad'm, I never did." She spoke decisively, almost angrily. "And I don't think I ever will. I got fed up living in the mountains with Pa when I was a kid. Nobody to talk to, no place to go, stuck in a cabin where there was nothing to do with, one day exactly like every other day—no, thank *you!* No more of that for me! And now with Benji—my goodness, Dear Mad'm, you aren't in earnest, are you?"

"It was just a thought," I said hastily, "and evidently not a good one. You see, I imagined you enjoyed your two visits with me—"

"Oh, I did!" she said hastily. "But a visit is different from settling down in a place for keeps. You understand that, don't you?"

"Of course," I said, and started to talk again of Benji, how cute he was and how pretty. But my heart was heavy. I loved both Nora and Up'nUp, and there seemed no chance of happiness for them. Up'nUp's youthful spirit would, I was sure, quickly shrivel and grow old in town, working indoors from nine to five. Nora's cramped and lonely childhood blinded her to the rich satisfactions of life close to nature. What would be the outcome? I could not guess.

After another look at Benji—asleep now—I went off to see the doctor for that checkup the magazine article declared I ought to have. He was the kind of doctor women fall for at first glance. Clean and fresh-looking, acting like you were the only patient of the day and yours the most interesting case he'd seen in weeks. When I told him I was past eighty, he made the perfect response. "You don't look it," he said, with just the right note of surprise in his voice. The dear! If he found out that I had high blood pressure, arthritis, and a ticker that was slightly imperfect, he didn't mention it. He put aside his instruments and looked at me with a smile.

"You go home," he said, "and be happy. Don't worry, don't lose sleep. Putter in your garden, have all the fun you can. Forget this old-age nightmare."

Just the looks of him sent my spirits soaring.

I went back to the station to catch the three-thirty bus. I felt as if I had stepped off a merry-go-round—a little dizzy with relief at what the doctor had said and quite happy— appropriately enough, since I was going to Happy Camp. There the boys would be waiting to take me home.

I climbed onto the bus, took the first vacant seat I came to, then looked off to the horizon. I didn't like the way the clouds were piling up from the south, nor the sudden gusts of wind that whished the dust of the street into little swirls and puffs. We had a young driver, a slim-faced youth of eighteen or so. He gazed at the sky and said worriedly to us passengers; "Looks as if we were in for a big storm."

Neither his words nor his manner contributed anything to my peace of mind. I hate to travel over mountain roads—especially the narrow ones we have in the Siskiyou mountains— when there's a storm of any proportions.

Beside myself and the driver, there were four other people in the bus. Across the aisle from me sat a distraught young woman who evidently wore her schoolteacher manners all day. Anyway, she had them on now. An uneasy young man squirmed on the seat ahead of me. Then there was the blank-faced Indian boy who had leaped on the stage from a shoe-shine stand in front of a barber shop. The other passenger was a sloppy, dough-faced young man who announced in a loud voice that he was part of a band—the main part, he wanted us to know. He had come aboard holding a huge instrument case over our dodging heads. "Soon as I hit my seat, I'll begin snoring," he said—and made good on that declaration. He looked so spongy that I felt like punching him down with my fist, as if he were a pan of dough.

By the time we pulled out on the highway, it had begun to sprinkle. A few miles farther along, when we were well into the mountains, the heavens opened up and let us have a deluge. The jittery young schoolteacher started to hold a conversation with herself—but intended for me to hear.

"I don't like this driver," she fumed. "He's going much too fast on this slippery pavement. Such careless driving!"

Apparently thinking she had not impressed me sufficiently, she leaned across the aisle and raised her voice.

"I've ridden with him a number of times," she informed me. "He's irresponsible. Aren't you frightened?"

I shook my head. What was the use owning up that I was, to a woman already in a panic? At that instant one of our fenders barely clipped a passing car. The young schoolteacher uttered a muffled screech.

"My, my! This is awful!" she chattered. "If I live to get to where I'm living, I'll never ride this bus again. I came from Alabama where they have trained, responsible bus drivers— ouch! What now?"

The old bus came to a jerky stop. The driver spoke over his shoulder in a boyish tenor.

"Something is wrong with the emergency brake. It won't work."

"It don't have to work," said the nervous man sitting in front of me. "Not if you go slow enough."

"Yes, yes, boy! Drive slow!" instructed the schoolteacher.

"Well, the other brakes ain't so good, neither," the boy confessed.

I was about to say, "I smell smoke," but held my tongue. Seemed like we had enough troubles without that.

The boy started the motor and we picked up speed on the slippery road. The bus skidded sickeningly, was brought back under control. The young lady from Alabama clutched her portfolio of lesson papers and sat on the edge of her seat.

"Driver, stop this bus!" she shouted. "Here's where I get off!" Her voice rose above the rattle of the old bus, and the sound of wind and pelting rain.

The boy came to a nice smooth stop on a bit of level road. He looked in wonder at the woman plunging down the aisle. He pulled the door open. She dropped down into the mud and slush at the edge of the pavement. The door swung shut behind her and we moved forward again.

"I don't know what's the matter with her, anyway," the boy complained. "Another five minutes and we'd have been at the rest station where she always gets off. I guess we're good for another half-mile."

The nervous young man in front of me turned.

"I tell you, madam," he said, "I'm not used to these narrow, winding roads and the harum-scarum drivers, and I don't like 'em."

I thought, if people on this bus don't stop acting like this, I'm going to get scared myself.

Through all this the Indian boy looked straight ahead, his face expressionless. The rain continued, and early twilight came down around us. This told me that the clouds were thick and heavily laden with water. Steadily we climbed Cade Mountain and came to a stretch of dirt road, now inches deep in mud. The bus slipped from side to side while the boy made desperate efforts to hit the ruts and stay in them.

We started down on the other side of the mountain. Our speed increased alarmingly, and the boy seemed to be engaged in a wrestling match with the emergency-brake lever. Smoke started to curl up through the floor boards. We all saw it and stared nervously at the door. If the bus burst into flames, would we be able to . . . we were going faster and faster.

Suddenly the driver ran the bus into the bank at one side of the road. We came to a jolting, shuddering halt. The doughy young man stopped snoring. The driver turned around and faced us.

"Here's where I stop for the night," he said, in the manliest voice I'd heard him use.

It was quite dark now. I drew my first deep breath in an hour. But my next thought was of the boys waiting for me in Happy Camp. What would they think when I did not arrive?

"Maybe we can do something about that brake," said the doughy young man, getting up and coming to the front of the bus. "I gotta play at a Happy Camp dance tonight. Won't be no band worth speaking about if I ain't there."

He and the driver climbed out. I heard them lighting matches and probing around under the raised hood. Even I knew this was an odd place to look for an emergency brake.

"Quit that, you fools!" the nervous young man shouted. "Use your flashlight!"

"I ain't got one," whimpered the boy.

"I have a flashlight—right here in my handbag." I gave it to the boy and he disappeared again into the darkness. The nervous young man alternately pounded and jerked on the emergency-brake lever.

"It's frozen," was his verdict.

"Looks more like it's on fire," I commented, gazing at the smoke that curled upward, now diminished in volume. The boy, looking like a drowned puppy, slid in the door and tossed the flashlight into my lap. It was plastered with mud and grease, and was badly battered. He had evidently been using it as a hammer.

The doughy-faced young musician came inside too. He and

the nervous young man went back to their seats. We sat in glum silence, waiting for something to happen, though there seemed no likelihood that anything would—when something did. The regular mail stage pulled carefully by us and stopped.

"Anything I can do for you?" shouted the driver.

"There's a lady here who'd like to go to Happy Camp."

The nervous passenger jumped to his feet. "I want to go too," he said decisively.

"Me, too," stated the stolid Indian boy, sidling into the aisle.

"I'll stay here with the driver," the fat young musician called out. "He might need someone to help him. Happy Camp'll just have to make out the best it can without me to-night."

He was a man, after all—right after my own heart. It's so easy to be deceived by appearances.

I was well-soaked by the time I got into the crowded rear seat of the mail stage. Where the nervous young man and the Indian boy sat I do not know.

"Are you all right, Grandma?" called the mailman over his shoulder. I assured him I was in fine shape. Now, that was the first time anyone had ever called me Grandma, except my one grandchild. As we rolled uneventfully along down the steep mountainside I was pondering. How in Sam Hill did that man know I was old enough to be a grandmother? It was pitch dark, and I hadn't uttered a word until I answered his question. I wished someone would enlighten me.

When we stopped in front of the small hotel in Happy Camp I saw the dripping figures of Dearsir and Up'nUp. As they helped me out of the mail stage, the mail carrier sang out, "Goodnight, Grandma. Hope you're none the worse for wear."

That man!

The boys took me to a small eating place. Perched on high stools, we had roast-beef sandwiches and hot coffee. While we ate the boys kept insisting that we see the picture of the Big Fight that was showing at the Del Rio Theater. They thought the rain was slackening off, and the worst of the storm would be over in the next hour or so. Then it would be safer to travel over that stretch of road along the bluff.

"You mean—that place where it rains rocks and mud slides in wet weather?" I asked, trying to keep the panic out of my voice.

"Now don't you worry," Up'nUp tried to reassure me. "There'll likely be no danger at all, time we get there. And we'll try to see that somebody with a heavier car than our jalopy goes ahead and pushes the rocks—if any—over the side and into the River, see?"

I didn't want to see. I'd been over that piece of road in daylight and it was beautiful then; the cliff draped and festooned with wild fuchsias, syringas, and azaleas, ferns and moss growing in the crevices—on the other side, far below, the roaring jade waters of the Klamath. But that was in sunlight. Tonight—in darkness and rain—well, that was different. I agreed to stay for the show.

Twenty-four

———◆◆◆◆———

W E MADE our way through the downpour to the Del Rio Theater. When we were seated, I between the two men, I poked Dearsir in the ribs. "Up'nUp said something about rocks in the road—"

"Pay no attention, Dear Mad'm. They only roll down when it rains, but by the time we get there it probably won't be raining. Up'nUp talks too much. And anyway, you know how he exaggerates."

Exaggerates? What if he did? Just one rock, if it were large enough and hit us just right, would roll the old jalopy off that shelf of a road and into the River.

"Maybe we'd better stay at the hotel—go home in the morning?"

"Sh-h-h-h!" hissed Up'nUp. "The show's beginning. There's Joe! Be quiet."

Silence fell over the crowded little theater. Several dignified gray-haired men with their wives sat near me in hushed expectancy. I looked about, wondering what it was that made sensible-looking, mature people so absorbed in what was going on up there ahead of us. My eyes followed theirs.

Why—this was exciting—this was terrific . . . I sat forward on the edge of my seat. A few minutes later I began to splutter hot, incoherent words. Dearsir pulled me back.

233

"Relax," he said. "This is only a picture, you know."

"It was real once!" I snapped back. "That man circling around is a panther—a black panther! Ah! He knocked Joe Louis down! One—two—three—he's up . . ."

A boy three rows behind us cheered. People around me made the air quiver with disapproval of the interruption. Stay hushed, boy—let the million-dollar ringside audience roar for blood! This is not the middle of the twentieth century. I felt the mad thirst for carnage that swept the crowds in the Coliseum long ago in Rome.

I was on the edge of my chair again—that black panther's a scamp—he's unbearable—he's got nice Joe Louis down again —Joe rises—the panther comes on—he's going to worst that baby-faced colored boy with the pouting lips—tut-tut, knock the beast down, Joe-boy . . .

Again I felt Dearsir's hand on my arm.

"Be still, Dear Mad'm. People are paying more attention to you than to the fight."

I sank back, ashamed—not of myself alone, but of all of us who could be so carried away by an exhibition of brutality. I kept quiet after that.

Finally the picture ended. Women pulled on their wraps, men got up stiff from sitting so long. Something hammered in my brain—words from a poem—what was it called, now . . . "American Prize Fight," that was it. I had read it long ago in the *Atlantic*. Fragments of it came back to me . . . "Let wisdom's muted trumpet once be heard, not idiocy's horn. Quick breath of shame . . ." Now I understood. The writer must have felt the same "quick breath of shame" that had swept over me when I realized how excited I had become.

Dearsir and Up'nUp leaned across me and talked in low voices.

"That man who lives below us on the River just left," Dearsir said. "He'll probably be pulling out soon. We better follow him. He can shove most of the rocks out of the road with that jeep of his."

"OK, let's beat it," agreed Up'nUp.

We went down the aisle toward the door, Dearsir's firm hand guiding me through the press.

"How'd you like it, Dear Mad'm?" he asked.

"I hate that black panther," I muttered, still in a quiver of excitement. "I wish Joe Louis had smashed his face."

Dearsir's grip tightened on my arm. "Now, Dear Mad'm, Jersey Joe was great. He had the Bomber whipped. The decision was a damned shame."

"It was all a damned shame!" I spat out the words. I had sat through a fight, hadn't I? So I could use ringside language if I wanted to, couldn't I? Anyway, I did.

Then we were outside. The rain was no more than a light, misty sprinkle. The boys decided it was safe to start home. Dearsir helped me into the car, which Up'nUp had driven close to the curb. I settled myself into the back seat. We drove out of the little hamlet into the blackness of the night. Ahead of us bobbed the taillight of the jeep—the boys had taken care to pull out just behind it.

We had covered perhaps a mile or so of our journey when suddenly the rain began to fall again, so hard that it beat a furious tattoo on the top of the car. The busy windshield wiper swished back and forth without pause. All thoughts of the spectacle I had witnessed in the theater left my mind. It raced forward to that stretch of road, no more than a narrow shelf, that twisted along between the cliff and the river.

Up'nUp attended strictly to the business of keeping the car in the middle of the muddy road. Once in a while the jalopy slewed sideways with a sickening lurch, but each time Up'nUp fought it back until the wheels sank again into the ruts made by the few cars that had passed earlier in the evening. Sometimes we lost sight of the red pinpoint that was the jeep's taillight as it disappeared around one of the endlessly repeated curves . . . then we would see it again.

Suddenly I noticed that both men were leaning forward, peering anxiously into the darkness ahead.

"This is it," Dearsir said in a low voice I knew I was not intended to hear. "I can't see whether there's rocks in the road or not—drive slow, will you?"

"I can't drive any slower and keep up with the jeep," Up'nUp said. "And I sure don't want to get very far behind him. In case we get in trouble—"

At that moment the jalopy hit a rock. It shuddered, bounced out of the ruts and slithered toward the edge of the road that practically overhung the Klamath River. When the wheels were not more than a foot from the brink, Up'nUp wrestled them back again. We crept forward for another twenty-five yards or so. Then something else happened.

We came to a scraping standstill as our front wheels hit a rock the size of a water bucket. Dearsir wiped the windshield with his fingers and tried to look through the murky glass. I stood up in the back and peered over Up'nUp's shoulder. All I could see was a short piece of sodden roadbed. No sign of the jeep's taillight. Had we lost it for keeps? And now we were halted by this rock . . .

The boys got out into the pouring rain. Tugging, hauling, sliding and rolling, they worked the boulder to the edge of the road, sent it plunging over the brink. Crashing sounds, then a faint splash came to our ears. The boys climbed back in. Before Up'nUp could start the car, a small avalanche of mud slid onto the road ten feet in front of us.

"Make a lunge at it," said Dearsir, "before any more comes down to cut us off."

The car lurched forward, throwing me back in the seat.

There was a bump—we were through the two-feet deep pile of mud. We moved forward.

"I've lost the jeep's taillight," said Up'nUp.

"I just saw the reflection of its headlights on the canyon wall up ahead of us," said Dearsir.

I know I am not a coward, but I have a vivid imagination. In rapid succession I saw a dozen pictures of things that might happen to us—all terrifying. There was a tenseness in the boys' voices, but they weren't giving the impression of being frightened, or even nervous. I got the idea that they were "facing the music." Well, I'd try to face it, too.

"Maybe we better pull up a little closer." I could sense Up'nUp's straining eyes and tight-shut lips. He felt the responsibility of getting us over an almost impassable road. I was carrying that responsibility, too—back-seat driving, I believe it's called—but gave myself the credit that so far I hadn't uttered a sound.

"Why not pull into that little cove right ahead?" suggested Dearsir. "We might wait there until the jeep's taillight shows up again."

Up'nUp turned into the cove and stopped.

"It'll be safe here, won't it?" I said in a voice that was hard to get out of my throat.

"Don't count on it," said Up'nUp. "If there should be a cloudburst up on this mountain—and there is, plenty of times—a regular wall of water might come down through this cove and wash us into the River."

Apparently Dearsir wasn't listening to him, but giving all his attention to the road ahead. Our ineffectual headlights broke the gloom ahead for about a hundred yards. Beyond that stretched impenetrable blackness. Dearsir spoke suddenly.

"There's the taillight. He probably stopped to shove a boulder out of the way."

We pulled out of the cove. The road ahead as far as I could see was liberally sprinkled with rocks—small ones, fortunately. But there was no telling what minute . . .

At that moment I lost control of my tongue—and my common sense too, apparently.

"Can't we start walking back toward Happy Camp?" I asked.

"Don't talk about walking on this road," said Dearsir. "No one could dodge those falling rocks. We're safer where we are."

"Yes—until a big one strikes us point blank," Up'nUp broke in.

"Shut up," said Dearsir gruffly. "No use scaring Dear Mad'm to death. This is damned bad—but it might be worse."

How could it be worse? I only wished the men would pray. "God help us" would be enough.

We came around a point and into a short stretch of almost straight road. The headlights showed glistening rocks that menaced every step of our way. Water poured from the heavens and out of each little crevasse of the mountainside. There was no way of missing the rocks. It was a hard job for Up'nUp to ease the wheels safely over and around them, keep them from bouncing the car over the brink and into the River. At last we saw the red taillight of the jeep bobbing along not far ahead. Then suddenly it was still. We watched for a moment.

"Good gosh!" Up'nUp cried. "What's that jeep driver doing, standing in the middle of the road waving his flashlight?"

"He's in trouble, that's what." Both men leaped from the car and started running down the road through the rain. In the mountains men don't wait to be asked to help. They head right for where they're needed. In a moment I lost sight of them.

The panic that swept over me when I realized I was alone in the car was close to insanity. I stood up, clutched the back of the seat in a spasm of fear. The whole cliff seemed to be dissolving. Rocks slithered across the road in the slimy mud, bounced off the top and hood. I knew for a surety that the next one would strike me on the head. I faced the fact that there was no one to help me—my life was in my own hands. And I wasn't going to let it slip away from me without a struggle.

All this took only seconds to happen. I heard myself muttering aloud. Then I knew I was not alone. God was with me. I was talking to Him.

Like a flash a prayer went through my mind as I was struggling to open the car door. It swung open and I fell to the ground. Scrambling up, I ran down the road, keeping as close to the cliff as possible. A rock as large as a toy balloon hurtled into the road directly in front of me. I stumbled over it—struggled up—kept running.

I had gone only a little way when I heard the men yelling at me. Then I lost my footing and sank in a heap on the road.

"Go back! Go back!" they were shouting. "You'll be killed!" They reached me, breathless, jerked me to my feet, dragged me to the car and shoved me into the back seat.

"What in God's name made you do that?" Up'nUp's voice shook. I didn't have breath enough to explain.

"Drive as fast as you dare," said Dearsir. "If we can get by that next point before another boulder decides to land on the road—"

"The jeep," I gasped. "What happened?"

"A boulder half as big as this car landed in the road in front of it," Dearsir explained. "It took all three of us to pry it over the bank. There were several crowbars in the jeep or we never could have done it."

We crept slowly forward.

"Dearsir," I said hesitantly, "I think—wouldn't you say the rain was slackening?"

"I'm sure it is," he said. "It would, now that we're just about over that cliff road."

A few minutes more and we *were* off that dangerous stretch. The red taillight of the jeep winked out of sight as the driver picked up speed. The road was still muddy, of course, but there were no more rocks on it.

Twenty minutes later Up'nUp stopped the car at the foot of my trail. The storm had passed on and no water was falling except from the dripping trees. The boys helped me up to my cabin. We went inside, where Vicki greeted us with exuberant joy. Dearsir built a fire in the stove and we peeled off our sodden outer garments. In a few minutes we were drinking hot coffee—not talking much. We had been through too much in too short a time. Death had crowded us.

After a while the men got up to go. Dearsir paused in the doorway.

"Dear Mad'm," he said, "I hope you are none the worse for it. Up'nUp and I have got used to looking out for you, and— and please—take good care of yourself."

Up'nUp, loquacious once more, broke in. "We pulled you through this knothole pretty good. You've been here close to eight months now. Been pretty rough sledding part of the time—but you're improving. It would have been awful if we'd let you kick off tonight."

"I'm tough, boys."

"Not too tough," said Dearsir, smiling a little. "I think you need us—and we need—well, a responsibility. Good luck and good night."

I sat at the table a long time after they had gone, drinking another cup of coffee. In the last two hours I had passed through the most terrifying experience of my long life. It wasn't luck that saved me. It was God.

Twenty-five

———◆•••◆———

WE GET a good deal of rain in the Siskiyous during the winter and early spring, with now and then a light snow. So our mountains are beautifully green, and the many springs and lovely streams pour their bright waters into the mighty Klamath all the year round. But a rainy day in our mountains is as beautiful in its way as a sunny one. Wisps of filmy cloud drift among the great pines and cling here and there to the peaks. The evergreens glisten with moisture and the madrone trunks and limbs turn to burnished copper. The close, intimate sound of rain on the tight walls and roof of a cabin has an unalloyed charm when inside there is warmth, the comfort of an old chair that creaks companionably when you move, books both new and old, and an adoring dog. How could anyone wish for more?

Of course there were many fair days when the sun shone, and as spring advanced sap began to rise, leaves to unfold, tiny green plants to push their heads through the damp earth. The dark pines hung pale green tassels of new growth on the tip of every branch. The boys took time off from washing gravel to put in a lavishly planned vegetable garden at Bent Pine and I began to think of what flowers I should plant in my front and back yards and on the two terraces. Bulbs and per-

ennials would come up of themselves, but the annuals had to
be replanted. I wrote letters to seed houses and got them off
via Tom and the mail stage.

March brought more fine days. The boys completed the
trail to the diggings. I went up several times to watch them
work for an hour or so, then made cautious side trips into the
forest to feast my eyes on the bright glory of redbud and the
prodigally blooming dogwood. Sometimes I found the rare
and delicate wild iris or the strange coral root pushing its rosy
head up through the sodden brown leaves and pine needles,
the whole plant looking like one exotic blossom.

The migrant birds came back, first singly, then in flocks. On
March 20, I saw the first buzzard of spring, effortlessly spiral-
ing high above me in great, slow circles.

In midmorning of one of these bright, almost effervescent
days, I was putting on my pink smock preparatory to planting
pansies on the second terrace, Vicki pacing impatiently, waiting for me to open the front door, when I heard a car stop at
the foot of my trail. Both Vicki and I knew it was not the boys'
jalopy. I opened the door—and there was Nora, Benji on one
arm, the other encircling a big thermos jug.

I greeted her with joy. She tumbled Benji on the bed, set
the thermos jug on the floor.

"I have to make another trip to the car," she said. "Watch
that scamp, will you, Dear Mad'm? Just to see that he doesn't
fall off the bed. He is beginning to creep a little now."

While she was gone Benji made valiant efforts to sit up and
succeeded just as Nora appeared, carrying an apple box that
seemed heavy, even for her. On top of the box lay a blanket,
pillow, and the bag for carrying baby's things that I had given
her. She lowered all this to the floor beside the thermos jug
and eyed the assortment dubiously.

"Benji and I came to have a picnic with you and the boys
at the mine," she said. "Up'nUp told me there was a trail lead-

ing up there now." She dragged Benji from too close proximity to the edge of the bed, shoved him over on his back. He lay there making happy gurgling sounds, waving his arms and legs wildly. Nora looked at him fondly.

"He's big for his age," she said pridefully. "Only seven months old, and look at him. The spittin' image of Up'nUp, too."

Beyond the baby's fair coloring, I could see no resemblance whatever. But then, who was I to judge? I wasn't Benji's mother.

"I hope you didn't have anything else you wanted to do today." She looked at me anxiously.

"No, nothing that can't wait."

"Well, let's get started." Her eyes went back to the box, the thermos jug, all the other stuff piled there.

"Nora," I began doubtfully, "do we have to take all that up to the mine?"

"I don't know what I can leave," she said, frowning. "There's eats in the box—I spent most of yesterday cooking up the things Up'nUp likes best. There's hot coffee in the thermos—Benji has to have the blanket and pillow. Gosh, Dear Mad'm, I never once thought how I'd get all this up to the mine! Can you beat that for stupidity? All I thought about was how much Up'nUp would like a chocolate cake—and the other stuff I brought. Now I don't know what to do."

She sat down on the bed, all her happy plans shattered, looking as if she might cry the next minute. She knew, as well as I did, that there was nothing we could do. She couldn't possibly carry all that—and Benji besides—up the trail, and I'd be lucky to get myself up there, without being responsible for anything more, even a chocolate cake. It looked to me like she'd just have to turn around and drive back to Yreka.

My unhappy thoughts were broken off by a harsh, unmusical sound from up on the mountain above my cabin. It wasn't far away—probably only a little way beyond my out-house.

"What's that?" Nora asked in a startled voice.

"Oh, nothing," I said absently, preoccupied with my concern over Nora's disappointment. Then I added automatically. "It's just Pete, the friendliest mule—"

I stopped short. A plan sprang, fully formed in my mind. Foolish, maybe. Imprudent, no doubt of it. But a plan, just the same.

"You wait here," I told Nora. Hurrying to the woodshed, I found the rope the boys had used to take me up to see my assessment work finished, and grabbed a handful of crushed barley. Hurrying up the trail at my top speed—which any self-respecting tortoise would have scorned as too slow for him—I found Pete munching on a patch of tender grass.

He looked up, swung his huge brown ears forward in my direction, evidently smelled the barley, and came close. I let him take the grain from my hand with his soft lips. As soon as he had the last grain, and I could use both my hands, I tied the rope around his neck and led him down to the front door. Nora stood there, holding Benji in her arms.

"What on earth, Dear Mad'm—"

"Put the thermos jug in the box, Nora, and pile the blanket and pillow on top," I said briskly. "Pete will haul it up that nice smooth trail for us. You can lead Pete and carry Benji. I'll walk behind and see that the box doesn't tip over. We're going to have our picnic after all."

"But, Dear Mad'm—that mule—"

"He happens to be Pete, the friendliest mule—but I said that before. Get a move on you, Nora. We haven't got all day. I know what I'm doing." Well, I hoped I did, anyway.

She went back into the cabin, came out staggering under the things she had brought with her, then went in again to get Benji. She rigged up a sort of harness for Pete out of the rope and attached it to the box. That done, Nora went ahead, carrying Benji and leading Pete, which worked very well. I followed, with nothing to do except keep my eyes on the box and now and then rake a stone out of its course.

When Dearsir saw our little procession he dropped the shovel he was using to dump gravel into the sluice box and ran to shut off the water from the Little Giant Up'nUp was aiming at a gravel bank. Both men strode up to us.

"What are you doing here?" Up'nUp demanded truculently of Nora.

"For God's sake, Dear Mad'm!" was Dearsir's astonished greeting. He seemed to be incapable of further speech.

"You boys run along back to your work," I said airily. "Don't mind us. We just came up for a picnic. Courtesy of Pete, the friendliest mule in the Siskiyous."

"Well, I'll be everlastingly hornswoggled!" was Up'nUp's contribution. "Nora, I've got a good notion—"

"I brought you a chocolate cake," Nora interrupted hastily. "Made it myself."

"You did?" Up'nUp's frown dissolved into a smile. "Where is it?"

"In the box, silly. Move it over into the shade of that tree."

Up'nUp sprang to do her bidding. Dearsir took the makeshift harness off Pete, gave him a slap on the rump. Pete ambled off into the brush. Nora and I spread the blanket, settled ourselves under the tree. The boys went back to work. I heard Nora sigh with contentment as she hugged Benji and leaned back against the tree trunk. I lay down, my head on Benji's pillow. These sudden excursions are fun, but a bit wearing, on even young legs such as mine.

When the shadows of the trees pointed due north the boys knocked off work. Nora and I took the food out of the apple box. We ate the tasty roast-beef sandwiches and potato salad she had brought, drank hot coffee poured from the thermos jug. Then came the chocolate cake, and I had to admit I had never tasted a lighter, tenderer or more delicious one. Nora, for all her occasional lapses into haphazard ways, could certainly cook.

"Not bad," said Up'nUp, finishing his third piece. Then he added, "And you ain't either, Nora."

Her face lit up with the happiness of a woman basking in the approval of her man. She clipped him a hearty blow on the ear.

"You big slob," she said. "You're not a total loss, yourself."

For them, this was utterly sentimental, completely lacking in restraint. I was immensely cheered. Maybe they'd yet find that their greatest happiness was in being together, as a man and woman who love each other should. In a burst of emotion I gave Vicki half of my second piece of cake. She made away with it in two ecstatic gulps.

The boys went up the gulch to inspect the flume. Nora packed up the picnic things, rocked Benji to sleep in her arms, then laid him gently on the blanket. She started for a walk, saying she was going to hunt for wild iris. I lay down beside Benji—and went sound asleep, for how long I have no idea.

I was awakened by the wild barking of Vicki close by one of the sluice boxes not fifty feet down the gentle slope. Scrambling to my feet, I looked wildly around. No one was in sight. With a sickening lurch of the heart, I realized that this included Benji. I plunged down toward Vicki, still pouring out her wild cries for help. At the same time I heard the heavy running footsteps of the boys racing down the gulch. I reached the sluice box— There was Benji face down, kicking and spluttering angrily in four inches of muddy water and gravel. I grabbed him by the straps of his blue denim play suit and dragged him to a sitting position. To save me, I couldn't lift the chubby little fellow out of the sluice box, but that wasn't important. All that really mattered was to get his face out of the water. He squirmed, fought and yelled, spit out gravel and mud. But I held on. Then Up'nUp leaned over, grabbed his son, hoisted him out. Nora came running, hurled herself on them and all three went down; Benji screaming, Nora crying over and over, "My baby! My baby!" Vicki circled them, barking joyfully. The noise was terrific.

Dearsir and I looked at each other and began to laugh, adding our shouts of glee to the bedlam.

When we had all calmed down, we figured out what had happened. Benji must have awakened, decided to do a little adventuring of his own. He probably crept part way, rolled the rest, until he was at the sluice box. A little investigation there and he was over the edge. If it had not been for Vicki sounding the alarm, he might easily have drowned in those scant inches of water.

This was a sobering thought, and suddenly no one felt like laughing any more. We were too deeply thankful that all had turned out well. Nora washed the gravel out of Benji's blond hair, took his play suit off and hung it on a limb. Up'nUp put a dry shirt and pants on Benji, the first time I had ever seen him do anything for the baby, and then held the child in his arms until Nora came to take him. He had a strange look on his face, I wished I knew what he was thinking. But I was certain that it took more wisdom than I possessed to figure Up'nUp out. As far as Nora and the baby were concerned, he had always been an enigma to me.

Finally the boys went back to work. At four o'clock they knocked off, helped carry Benji's things and what was left of the picnic down the trail to my cabin. Nora left soon afterward. She had a long drive ahead of her and wanted to get home before dark. Up'nUp went down to the car with her, carrying Benji, his blanket and pillow. Dearsir and I sat in the kitchen.

"What do you suppose will happen to those two?" I asked, feeling very low in my mind about them.

"I couldn't even guess," Dearsir returned soberly. "As I told you once a long time ago, Dear Mad'm, I don't know anything about matrimony—most of all, the kind they've got. I'm plain stumped. Looks like, no matter what they do, it won't turn out right."

"What do you mean?"

"Well, if he gives up living in the mountains, goes to Yreka to stay with Nora and Benji, he'll end up no good to them or himself, either. He just naturally wasn't born for town life. And if Nora should, by some unheard-of chance, come to live with him on the Klamath, she'll be mighty unhappy. And they're both unhappy the way things are. You figure that one out, Dear Mad'm. I sure can't."

"I can't either—except by a miracle."

"I don't say there's never been a miracle," Dearsir said slowly, "but I've never seen one on the Klamath." He rose. "I better be going along," he added. "Up'nUp's evidently gone on up to Bent Pine."

"When are you boys going to have a cleanup?"

"Oh, soon now. Sometime around the second week in April, probably."

"How do things look? Will it be a good one, do you think?"

"Hard to tell, Dear Mad'm. Sometimes a cleanup turns out better than we hoped. Sometimes it's real disappointing. No way of telling ahead of time. Well, I'll probably see you tomorrow. Take good care of yourself."

After he was gone Vicki came and laid her head in my lap, looked up at me with her beautiful brown eyes. I patted her.

"Vicki," I said, "I love Nora and Up'nUp so much and I'm so troubled about them. I don't know whether I can go on taking it or not. I'm downright unhappy here. So why do I stay? Why don't I pick up and go back to San Francisco?

I've been here almost a year now—nobody could say I'm a quitter—"

But Vicki was bored with all this. She turned away, lay down on the cougar rug by my bed, gave a great sigh and went to sleep.

I decided to have a bowl of hot soup and go to bed. Maybe things would look brighter in the morning. But I didn't really think they would.

Twenty-six

———◆◆◆◆———

WHEN morning came my gloomy thoughts of the night before turned out to have been prophetic or something—maybe more of that woman's intuition that most of the time I don't take much stock in. The boys stopped in on their way to the mine and, beyond a sober "good morning," wordlessly accepted the coffee I poured for them. I could see they had something on their minds, and whatever it might be, was plainly no cause for rejoicing.

"Something gone wrong at the mine?" I asked.

"No, everything's fine up there," Dearsir responded, taking a cautious sip of the steaming coffee.

"Have you missed any more nannies?"

"Nary a one," Up'nUp said. "You put a stop to that, Dear Mad'm, when you killed the cougar, remember?"

I tried again.

"How's Pete?"

"Fat and sassy," Dearsir reported. "Saw him yesterday up above the nannies' barn."

I ran out of patience, always in moderately short supply with me. "Then what in time's the matter with you?" I asked.

Dearsir looked at Up'nUp. Up'nUp stirred his coffee. Finally Up'nUp spoke.

"I've decided to quit messing around with gold mining," he said. "It's the bunk. I got a wife and child—"

So that was it.

"You've had a wife and child for quite a while," I said mildly. "So what brought this on?"

"Yesterday brought it on," Up'nUp said. "I think I've been one of them retarded adolescents the magazines you and Dearsir take are always talking about."

"My goodness, Up'nUp! What on earth do you mean?"

He shook his head. "I guess I never really felt like I was a father until I dragged Benji out of that sluice box. Or maybe it was when I was running down the hill, afraid he was drowned. And as for Nora—well, she needs me around to help bring up the kid."

"Look, Up'nUp," I said, "those are extremely noble reasons for giving up the life you love. Just a little too noble for everyday use. If you haven't any others, you'd better—"

"I got others," he interrupted me. "Nora, she—well—I kinda like her. And Benji—he's a first-rate kid. Plain truth is, Dear Mad'm, I been missing a lot, not being with 'em, and I don't aim to miss no more."

"Well, that's better," I said. "I hope you realize, though, that it's going to be different, taking a job in town."

"Yeah," he said. Then he added doggedly, "But I guess I can stand it."

I looked anxiously at Dearsir. The expression on his face did nothing to reassure me.

"I suppose you'll go on to Yreka tomorrow and tell Nora," I said. Up'nUp shook his head.

"Can't make it. We're close to the cleanup. When that's over will be plenty of time."

"He's going to leave his share of the claims for me to take care of," Dearsir said. "I'll have to find somebody to help me. Maybe one of Millie's cousins. They're good, steady boys." He rose. "I'm going to hang on. Personally, Dear Mad'm, I think he'll be back. I give him six months."

"The very idea! Don't you say such a thing!" My remark was addressed to myself as much as to Dearsir, for I was thinking the same thing. But I didn't want it to come out that way, because I loved Nora and Benji so much.

"Sorry," Dearsir muttered. "Come on, Up'nUp. Let's get on the job."

They went up the trail and I was left to my thoughts—very unhappy and unsettling they were, too.

Then, for the first time, I realized what Up'nUp's leaving would mean to me. I would not only lose Up'nUp—I would also lose Nora and Benji. I wouldn't be hearing about them as I had after each of Up'nUp's visits to them, and they wouldn't be coming to Bent Pine any more. The trip to Yreka was too much of a jaunt for me to take often. This would be the end of any close friendship between us. Only Dearsir would be left. I sighed drearily.

The days of spring went by. In my back yard the fruit trees burst briefly into lovely bloom, then scattered the petals like pink snow. By looking closely I could see the tiny green balls that the summer sun would bring to colorful beauty and juicy deliciousness. Trillium and the fairylike columbine blossomed everywhere in the forest. Along the edges of countless tiny rills, tender, tangy watercress flourished. It was a lovely time, but I found only brief moments of pleasure in it. With Up'nUp gone, life would be different. My thoughts drifted more and more often to San Francisco.

The second week in April the boys stopped washing gravel and went to work picking the larger nuggets out of the sluice boxes. That done, they removed the burlap lining of the sluice boxes and let it dry out. Then they burned it, leaving the gold dust in the ashes. At last they were ready to recover and weigh the result of two months' work. I wanted to go up to Bent Pine and watch them, but they pointedly did not invite me. Well, I didn't blame them—I would be sure to poke around asking questions. So Vicki and I stayed home. I spent a restless, unhappy day—couldn't even settle down to working in my garden.

Next morning, just as I was putting the coffee pot on the stove, there came a knock at my front door.

"Come in!" I called, thinking it was the boys. To my surprise, Tom stepped inside.

"An airmail, special delivery letter," he said, holding it out. "Lots of airmails come, but I don't very often get a special delivery. Hope it isn't bad news."

I hurriedly tore the letter open. Who on earth would be sending me an airmail, special delivery letter? And why?

I read the first line and knew it was not bad news, turned to the end, saw that the letter was signed by five of my relatives in San Francisco—a sort of round robin.

"Just birthday greetings from my family," I said. "What date is this, Tom?"

"The thirteenth of April. So this is your birthday—"

"No, tomorrow. I'd forgotten about it."

"Many happy returns, Mrs. Patterson. I'm glad the letter wasn't bad news. Goodbye."

"Thank you for bringing it up. Goodbye, Tom."

I sat down and read the letter. The farther I read the worse I felt. Why didn't I come back? they asked. Why did I persist in living so far away from them all? And in the wilds of Siskiyou County, at that? At my age. Do come back—we'll get your house in order for you—we'll see that you are taken everywhere you want to go—we'll do everything possible to keep you comfortable, entertained, amused, happy. Etc., etc., etc.

My heart went out to them in gratitude for their love, their unselfish devotion. But they were concerned only with what they could do for me. There wasn't one word about what I could do for them. They didn't need me. Their lives were full and busy. They had no need for an old woman who would be eighty-one tomorrow. I would fill no gap in their lives. I would just be an appendage, a recipient of favors—lovingly planned and given, to be sure, but still one-way affairs.

However, I asked myself, would I be any more needed here, with Nora, Up'nUp and Benji out of my life—only Dearsir left? I might as well face it—there was very little I ever had done, or ever could do, for Dearsir. He was always doing things for me. And in San Francisco I would be wrapped in every comfort . . .

My thoughts went round and round as aimlessly as a wheel in a squirrel cage, getting nowhere, reaching no new goal. I would go—I would stay—I would go—I would stay . . .

Unbearable. I jumped up, put on my coat and started for Bent Pine, Vicki at my heels. If I hurried I might catch the boys before they left for Happy Camp with their gold from the clean up. I'd tell them about the letter, ask them—well, I didn't know exactly what. But just to talk to them would help.

When Vicki and I came to Bent Pine the boys were sitting down to breakfast.

"Come in!" Dearsir called. "We worked late last night, so we overslept. Otherwise we'd have been gone by now. Will you have hot cakes and ham with us?"

Not until then did I remember that I had come away without my breakfast.

"I certainly will," I said, seating myself at the table. My spirits rose at the prospect of Dearsir's pancakes. There was a great sizzling as Up'nUp poured batter on the griddle with a generous hand. Dearsir filled my coffee cup.

"How did the cleanup come out?" I asked.

"Fair to middling. Could have been worse, could have been better. Round three thousand. Enough so I won't run out of beans for a while. And Up'nUp—he'll have a little breathing spell so as he can look around for a job in Yreka—won't have to take the first one that offers."

"After we get the gold to the express office at Happy Camp," Up'nUp volunteered, flipping my plate-sized pancake over, "I'm going on to Yreka to—well, to tell Nora."

"You going to stay there?" I asked Up'nUp with a sinking sensation.

"Not today. I'll be back. Got to help Dearsir for a week or so."

Up'nUp put the giant pancake on my plate and topped it with a piece of delicately browned ham the size of his hand.

"You're looking kind of down in the mouth, Dear Mad'm," he said. "What you got on your mind?"

Between bites of ham and pancake I told the boys about the special delivery letter.

"What are you thinking of doing?" Dearsir asked, looking down at his plate.

"I guess I might as well go back to San Francisco," I said drearily. "Looks like it's the sensible thing to do. Everything seems sort of—well—changing, here. After all, as they say, it's pretty silly, at my age—"

I was interrupted by a rumbling sound of some heavy vehicle coming down the roadway to the cabin. It stopped with a screech of brakes.

"Hi!" a woman's voice called. "Get out here, you two big lummoxes. We're going to need help. Step on it, will you?"

Nora's voice. We looked at each other wildly. We scrambled to the door. Dearsir flung it open.

There stood Nora, grinning at us, Benji in her arms. Behind her loomed a truck, its bulky load hidden under a tarpaulin.

"Do I stop here, or pull ahead?" asked the driver.

"Just don't do nothing for a bit. Wait till I break the news to them," Nora replied.

"Nora!" thundered Up'nUp. "You—what's in that truck?"

"Sh-h-h. Take it easy," Nora said, nervously patting Benji's fat leg. "I—well—I hope you won't mind, Up'nUp—but that's our furniture—and a tarpaulin to go over it until you can build a cabin for Benji and me—for us, I mean—and a tent for us to live in until the cabin is ready . . ." She seemed to run down. None of us said anything—just stood staring at her. I had never seen Nora look uncertain before. As I watched, her uncertainty turned to fright.

"Up'nUp," she said, and waited. He was silent. "Well," she said finally, "if you don't want us, we can go back, I guess. I haven't rented the house yet—"

He glowered at her. "I don't get it," he said. "You mean you came down here—to *stay?*"

Nora glanced appealingly at Dearsir, then at me. Neither of us spoke or moved. Even the man on the seat of the truck might have been carved out of stone. This was between her and Up'nUp.

Some of her old spirit came back to her.

"Of course I came intending to stay, silly! I figured I'd see a lot more of you—and Benji would, too. A part-time father's no good to any kid. And everything would be different than when I lived on the Trinity River with Pa. There'd be Dear Mad'm to keep me company, and—"

A grin broke over Up'nUp's face. "Aw, gee, Nora! Gosh, that's swell! What do you know! Me—I was going to Yreka today to tell you I'd come there to live—"

"Of all the stupid things I ever heard! You'd never be happy in a town. I saw that the day Benji and I were up at the mine."

"But you won't be happy here."

"Oh, yes, I will. You'll see. That is—if you—"

"Say, lady," the truck driver broke in, looking completely bored, "if you'll just tell me whether I'm to unload this stuff, or take it back to Yreka—"

Up'nUp took charge. "Just pull up about fifty feet," he directed. "We'll lay some boards on the ground and pile the furniture on top. Step back out of the way—no, the women, not you, Dearsir; you lend a hand here."

The truck driver did as he was told. Nora handed Benji to me and I sat down on a bench to watch. Nora carried boards, helped lift tables, beds, rolls of carpet. In a short time the empty truck turned around, headed back up the road. Up'nUp, Dearsir and Nora put up the wall-tent Nora had brought, placed a bed, table, dresser, and two chairs in it. Then they stretched the tarpaulin over the rest of the furniture and tied it down as a protection from the spring rains.

It all happened so fast that I didn't fully realize the significance of it all. Nora and the men came back to the cabin, Up'nUp took Benji from me. We went inside and sat down.

The quiet was extraordinary. It was like being in the eye of a hurricane after the turmoil, activity and confusion of the last hour. We weren't even thinking of the readjustment in all our lives that would have to be met and dealt with almost immediately.

The peace didn't last long. Up'nUp began to frown.

"Nora," he said, "you're the wildest, craziest wife a man ever had. How are we going to buy lumber for a cabin? I'll bet you never gave that a thought. Dearsir and I had only a fair cleanup. Me and you and Benji can't live in a tent very long—only till early fall, at the latest—"

"Well, I've given it something that will pass for a thought, until something better comes along," Nora retorted. "I've got two thousand dollars in the Yreka bank, saved from when I was working for the telephone company—"

"Hooray! That ought to do it."

"And what's more," Nora went on as if Up'nUp hadn't spoken, "remember, I told you that I hadn't rented our house?

I've got a buyer for it, just waiting for us to sign the papers. Now am I the craziest—"

"No," Up'nUp said, with a look of admiration. "I'll admit I've known crazier."

"If you want to," Nora went on, "you can take the money from the house and buy—well, whatever it takes to work the mine on a somewhat larger scale, at any rate. You and Dearsir always been yelping about how you wanted to do that."

"Nora," Dearsir said in a voice that held both surprise and a kind of awe, "I take back everything I ever thought about you."

"Thanks, Dearsir." Nora's eyes sparkled. "I wish Up'nUp would say nice things to me like you do."

An hour passed and we settled down a little after all the excitement. The boys went off to Happy Camp with the gold, saying they'd be back by suppertime. I told them to come to my cabin and we'd eat there.

"Please bring some fancy food," I said. "If there is such to be had in Happy Camp. Seems to me this calls for a celebration."

After the boys were gone, Nora, Benji and I went down to my cabin and did nothing for the rest of the day. We talked part of the time, and part of the time we sat in companionable silence. Benji went to sleep on my bed, sweet and good and happy. I didn't bother about my problems—I didn't think about anything—except how happy I was that Nora and Up'nUp had found a solution to their problem, one I felt sure would bring happiness to them both—and to dear little Benji. As for me, well . . .

"Dear Mad'm," Nora said, "I never could have done it if you hadn't been here. I'm like the boys—I depend a lot on you."

"Depend on me! That doesn't make sense, Nora. I depend

on *them*. They're always doing something for me. Why, how can you say—"

"I don't know as I can explain it," Nora said, frowning. "But—well, it means a lot, just that you're here. You're kind of like—like you were part of the family—oh, I said I couldn't explain. I'll ask Dearsir. He says things better than I can."

Well, I understood—sort of—about the boys, but Nora— What she would need me for was a mystery.

Benji woke up and we talked of other things. Evening came and with it the boys, back from Happy Camp. We gathered in the kitchen to inspect what they had been able to secure in the way of the fancy food I had requested. There was a chocolate cake from the little bakery, two cans of tiny peas—the kind Dearsir liked so well—lettuce, tomatoes, a bottle of French salad dressing. Then came Up'nUp's proud contribution, four huge, thick, wonderful steaks. I remembered the time Nora had brought such steaks and Up'nUp's outspoken disapproval of her extravagance. Oh, my, I thought in dismay. I hope she won't remind him . . .

I need not have worried.

"Oh, Up'nUp, they're grand!" she exclaimed. He grinned, patted her cheek. I knew that the strange battle that had been waged between them was over.

"Just one more thing," Up'nUp said, fumbling in the box that had held the groceries. He drew out a can of mushrooms. "You wanted fancy food, Dear Mad'm," he went on, "and you sure got it."

"You're right. No one could have done better than you have," I conceded heartily.

We cooked dinner together, everyone lending a hand in my tiny kitchen, working in happy confusion. After dinner was over and the dishes washed, my guests lingered on and on as though reluctant to end this day. It was as if we all felt that we had reached a milestone in our lives, at once an end and a beginning. The boys said nothing about the letter from San Francisco, nor of our talk that morning, and I was glad. I didn't yet know what decision I would reach regarding it, and I wanted nothing to mar the happiness of this day.

Nora turned to Dearsir. "You know, I was trying to tell Dear Mad'm why we need her—why we depend on her. But I'm dumb when it comes to words. You tell her."

"That's very simple," he said, smiling. "Up'nUp and I need her because she needs us. Nobody can get along very well unless they're needed by someone. But Nora, you've complicated matters."

"Who, me?" Nora exclaimed. "Why, I never—"

"Oh, yes, you have," Dearsir said, serious now. "You and Benji will be at Bent Pine from now on. You're going to need Dear Mad'm as a friend and companion. Benji's going to need her for the special kind of love she has for him—different from the love of a father or mother—or even that of a kind of step-uncle like me. Benji and you are *really* going to need her. Isn't that so?"

"It sure is," Nora said fervently.

My goodness, I thought, they're talking about *me* . . .

"I think we better go now." Dearsir rose. "It's after eleven. We're going to be pretty busy from now on. And Dear Mad'm's got her work cut out for her, too." He turned, looked directly at me. "Haven't you, Dear Mad'm?" he asked.

I knew that his question held a depth of significance only he and I understood.

"Yes," I said steadily. "I have my garden to plant and take care of, you boys to be dependent on, Nora to talk to, and Benji to help bring up in the way he should go. Oh, yes, I have plenty to do here in the Siskiyous, and I intend to do it."

"Good!" he said. "That's what I thought you would say. Up'nUp, you going to carry Benji?"

Good nights were said and they went down the trail in the starlight, accompanied by the ever-present chant of the great River rushing tumultuously past.

Long after they had gone I sat at the kitchen table, drinking coffee, Vicki lying at my feet. The calendar on the wall showed that this day was the thirteenth of April. The clock said that in seven minutes more it would be midnight—and I would be eighty-one years old.

My decision was made. I would continue to live here in my little cabin, within sight and sound of the Klamath River. Here was the life I wanted—the life I loved. Flowers to fill my days with beauty, Vicki to protect me, and my dear friends at Bent Pine who depended on me—who needed me. My days would be full and happy, with the deepest satisfactions life can offer.